Ruth

The Mountains Sing

God's Love Revealed to Taiwan Tribes

BY RUTH WINSLOW

Includes Alice Hayes Taylor's Mountain Experiences

Light and Life Press
Winona Lake, Indiana 46590

Printed in the United States of America
by Light and Life Press
Winona Lake, Indiana 46590

ISBN 0-89367-094-4

Cover photos: Mountain scene by Jim Nelson; Paiwan child by Evelyn Mottweiler; Peng Chih-ting by Marian Groesbeck.

Back cover art: James Pai, artist of Taiwan

Contents

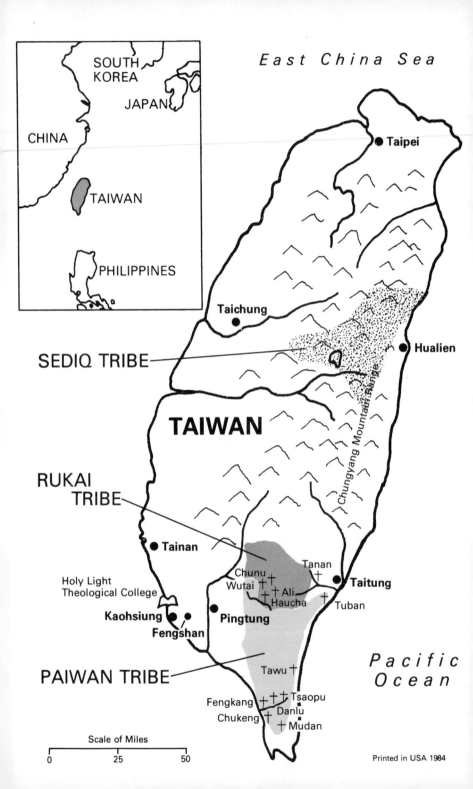

For my mother,
Evangeline Smith,
who inspired me
with courage

Pronunciation Guide
A partial list

Names of Places

Ali	(Ah' lee)	Mudan	(Moo' dahn)
Chukeng	(Choo' Kung)	Pingtung	(Ping' dohng)
Chunu	(Joo' new)	Taitung	(Ty' dohng)
Danlu	(Dahn' loo)	Taiwan	(Ty' wahn)
Fengkang	(Fung' gong)	Tanan	(Dah' nahn)
Fengshan	(Fung' shahn)	Tawu	(Dah' woo)
Haucha	(How' chah)	Tsaopu	(Tsah'-oh boo)
Hualien	(Hwah' lee an)	Tuban	(Doo' bahn)
Kaohsiung	(Gow' shung)	Wutai District	(Woo' ty)

Names of Tribes or Groups

Hakka	(Hah' kuh)	Sediq	(Suh' dik)
Paiwan	(Py' wahn)	Tayal	(Ty' ul)
Rukai	(Roo' guy)		

Names of People

Ba	(Bah)	Li	(Lee)
Chen	(Chun)	Loh	(Low)
Chi-oang	(Jee' wahng)	Ou	(oo)
Chu	(Joo)	Peng Chih-ting	(Pung' jih-ding)
Du	(Doo)	Tang	(Dahng)
Huang	(Hwahng)	Wang	(Wahng)
Hsieh	(Shih'-eh)	Wu	(Woo)
Hsieh Chi-chih	(Shih'-eh jee-jih)	Wufeng	(Woo-fung)
Kuo	(Gwuh)		

Introduction

This book is about Taiwan, yet it is not about the Taiwan that most tourists from the West visit. It is not about the Taiwan in news periodicals, nor about the eighteen million people that live on one third of the island. This book doesn't tell about booming industrialization, polluted cities, which are as ugly as the countryside is beautiful, or the excitement of an economy with little unemployment. Nor does it tell of nuclear power plants or mass transit systems with electrified railways. Neither is it a study for church growth specialists or missiologists.

Rather, in response to a request by the Women's Missionary Fellowship International to write a study book on the beginnings of the Free Methodist mountain work in Taiwan, I have written about the men and women who brought Christ to their own people. I have begun with the earlier period of time when headhunting was still a part of the mountain culture.

I have written of the little Sediq tattooed lady who found Christ and took the message to her own people high in the inner recesses of the mountains, beyond the barbed wire barriers of the Japanese.

The movement to Christ began with individuals, moved to clan and family groupings, then to whole villages within that tribe. By the postwar period of 1949, there were seven thousand baptized believers. I regret that this story cannot tell more of the remarkable growth which the Presbyterian Church has experienced, as there are now more than sixty-seven thousand members in five tribal presbyteries.

In the early 1950s, some of the Free Methodist missionaries who had served in China moved to Taiwan, centering their work in the southern cities of Pingtung, Fengshan, and Kaohsiung. These missionaries became aware of the unreached tribes in the nearby mountains. Because of the barriers of mountains and different languages, the gospel did not spread freely from tribe to tribe. In this story I have recounted how John Hsieh, Paul Kuo, and others of the Paiwan tribe led by Alice Taylor took the gospel to the villages along the South Cross-Island Highway and into the low foothills.

At approximately the same time, Peng Chih-ting of the Rukai tribe was converted. God led him to our church in Fengshan where young Paiwan mountain men were being given a short-term study of the Bible. He joined them and subsequently in God's timing took the gospel back to his own people in the Wutai District. Harry and I have been privileged to work closely with Pastor Peng. We have spent many hours on the trail with him hiking to remote mountain villages. He has inspired us with his love for the Lord and dedication to see everyone in his tribe know about Christ. Thus I hope my readers will capture the spirit of this man in the book.

Because it is a missions study book, and because God led Harry and me into a ministry to the mountain people in 1967, I have included in the third part excerpts from the years I was involved in a compassionate ministry to the mountain people. Harry was assigned by the annual conference of the China (now Taiwan) Free Methodist Church to serve in an advisory capacity to our young mountain churches. It was my privilege to accompany him to our Rukai villages for clinics and church-related trips.

After our first furlough in 1970, Harry no longer worked full time with the mountain churches, but as principal and teacher at Holy Light Theological College in Kaohsiung. I continued working however in a public health nursing capacity to the Rukai tribe until our third furlough in 1982. I am grateful to Harry who knew my love for the mountain people and supported me with

8

his thoughts and prayers, even when he was unable to go along. I'm grateful, too, for our four sons, Glenn, Mark, Keith, and Rodney, who took great delight in accompanying us, when they could, to share in our work for the Lord.

Most of all, I am thankful for the mountain Christians who have been a constant challenge to me in the Christian faith and who have given me far more than I could give them. It is my hope that the readers of this book will see the love of God that each national has for his own people, and will praise God with me that now the mountains sing of His love.

It is also my fervent prayer that as you read this story, you will feel committed to pray for these people who are still alive, working, and singing for the Lord in their mountain villages.

Ruth Winslow

The mountains sing.

9

Part I

To the Paiwan Tribe

Paiwan children enjoy wearing their tribal dress.

Chapter 1

In the Darkness of the Moon

The head rolled out of the bag. The mighty men's glee turned to dismay as they recognized a friend instead of a foe. Instantly their horror turned to sad wails, and they beat their chests and pounded their foreheads on the slate courtyard. Word of mouth quickly passed the dreadful news throughout the whole area that their close friend and helper from the plains had been killed in their ambush in the darkness of the moon.

This story of Wufeng has become a password, told from grandmother to son to grandchild, and forever passed on in the lore of the mountains in Taiwan. It is a true story.

Wufeng was a Taiwanese merchant who saw potential in trading with the mountain people. He was a kindly man and always fair in his dealings and trade. Certain items like salt and cloth could be purchased only on the plains. Little cash was available to these interior tribesmen; thus it was necessary to trade what they produced on the mountain slopes — millet, delectable mushrooms grown on the sides of trees, goat meat, exotic plants and orchids, and deer antlers for Chinese medicine. How easy it was for the plains' merchants to trade unfairly with the illiterate and seemingly ignorant mountain people.

Wufeng was well received, not only because of his fairness in business, but because he helped the people

13

in other ways. He settled close and lived in peace with them. Wufeng had a gentle, loving nature. He abhorred the violence that took place yearly as the tribal ceremonial rites were celebrated, and heads taken for these rites. He often spoke to the tribesmen about this evil practice; and because he was so helpful to them, their confidence and respect in his opinions rose.

One day as the men were sharpening their knives to hunt the wild boar for the feast of the harvest festival, they discussed the other hunt that would take place after the meat was in for the village. Wufeng joined the village fathers. As usual they were attentive and polite to all his ideas for their welfare.

"There is one thing you must stop, completely and forever," he said. "You must stop this practice of taking human lives in order to obtain heads. Every time you kill someone from another tribe, the others kill someone from your tribe. You are actually killing your own loved ones every time you kill an enemy." There was plenty of negative response to that from the village fathers. They felt sorry that they would have to grieve their respected friend. Finally, after much talk, they went to Wufeng and said that they would take only a few heads this year.

Wufeng was discouraged and showed grief at their decision. Not wanting to offend him, they gathered again and talked some more. Finally, the decision was made. They would take only one head.

Wufeng reluctantly accepted their decision. "If you take one head, can this be the last head you will ever take?" he asked. They promised.

"Then tell me," he asked, "where will you get your victim and when?" Trusting him, they told Wufeng the time and place of the ambush. He was thankful that he had their promise to stop head-hunting. Government officials would be happy that this one village, at least, was going to abandon the practice.

Preparations for the feast continued. The boar was cleaned for roasting, the millet dumplings prepared, the festive garments laid out, and the spears sharpened. Wufeng returned to his home with a final promise that just one head would be taken.

As the warriors left the village for the place of ambush, their enthusiasm ran high. On bare feet they noiselessly slipped to the place in the mountains where they could hide behind jagged rocks. The unsuspecting traveler would hear nothing or see nothing as the moon went behind the clouds.

Footsteps approached. As the moon became its darkest, the men stepped out from behind the rocks and took their victim.

Racing back to the village with the basket, they laughed and joked. Moments later their joy turned to horror as they saw the head they had taken.

Their Taiwanese friend, the only person that had truly cared for them, had knowingly become their sacrifice. He had made them promise to take only one more life, and he was that life.

The words of their leader were grim and determined, and all the people nodded assent. "We shall never forget our promise not to take another head."

Wufeng, the Taiwanese merchant and helper to the mountain people, gave his life so that head-hunting would come to an end in that mountain village in Taiwan. He died in the darkness of the moon, August 10, 1769.

Wufeng's act of bravery made a lasting impression on the mountain tribes and helped pave the way for Christianity which would follow. His story has been likened to the Lord Jesus, who gave his life so that all men might be free from sin.

Descendants of headhunters, these mountain men now prize boar skulls instead of human ones.

Chapter 2

Ilha Formosa, Beautiful Isle

Where was Wufeng from? What were the origins of this unusual Taiwanese man whose story is a password to the mountain people today in Taiwan?

In his time Taiwan was called Formosa. It was so named by a Portuguese skipper in 1590 who was plying his galleon in the Pacific Ocean. When he saw the green clad mountains, with peaks piercing the clouds, cascades of waterfalls glimmering like silver in the tropical sunlight, and terraced plains waving with feathery bamboo, he exclaimed, "Ilha Formosa," meaning beautiful isle. Thus it became known to its European conquerors over the centuries. To the Chinese who began arriving in the early seventeenth century, it was called Taiwan, meaning bay of terraces.

Taiwan stands for the island's two largest tribes: "Tai" representing the larger Tayal tribe located in the central and northeast mountains, and "wan" for the Paiwan tribe located in the southeast mountain range.

The eastern shore has rugged beauty. Magnificent cliffs rise out of the sea to a height of fifteen hundred to twenty-five hundred feet. They stand as a mighty bulwark in the sparkling blue of the Pacific Ocean. Two long mountain chains, with forty-eight peaks towering above eleven thousand feet, occupy the central and eastern backbone of Taiwan.

Contrasting the rugged mountain terrain, which occupies two-thirds of the island, is a twenty-five-mile-wide fertile plain. It stretches along the western coast, with wide river deltas emptying into the sea. Their origins lie in the mountains where mountain springs, rivulets, and streams converge to form the rivers. Situated in the ordinary course of typhoons, the island yearly bears the brunt of storms and typhoons. Because the mountains are steep and the creeks short, floods bring annual catastrophe.

Below usually azure skies are varieties of palms, broad-leafed bananas, flowering flame trees, and broad expanses of rice fields. Against this backdrop of green, majestic mountains rise in the distance along the entire 250-mile length of the island.

From the fertile coastal plains to the terraced hillsides, the vegetation gradually changes. The hills become mountains with moss-strung trees. Butterfly orchids nestle in the branches and provide a home for brilliantly colored birds. Rose-pink azaleas, lilies, and rhododendron splash the mountainsides. At the alpine elevation of six thousand feet the vegetation again changes to camphor laurel, tree fern, and giant benihi trees. Bubbling waterfalls tumble over rocks bordered by moss and lichen. The craggy peaks of the taller mountains are sparsely covered with pines and short grass. Here the hawks build their nests and soar out over the broad expanse of mountains and valleys from north to south. They view it all as one great island pearl lying in a sea of blue.

No wonder the first Canadian Presbyterian missionary, George Leslie MacKay, wrote in 1895, after having lived in Taiwan for twenty-three years:

Far Formosa is dear to my heart. On that island the best of my years have been spent. There the interest of my life has been centered. I love to look up to its lofty peaks, down into its yawning chasm, and out on its surging sea. I love its dark-skinned people, Chinese, Pepohoan, and savage, among whom I have gone these twenty-three years, preaching the gospel of Jesus. To serve them in the gospel I would gladly, a thousand times over, give up my life. . . . There I hope to spend what remains of my life, and when my day of service is over I should like to find a resting place within the sound of its surf and under the shade of its waving bamboo.[1]

The mountain "savages" of whom he speaks today comprise less than 1 percent of the total island population of eighteen million, and yet these tribes occupy more than half of the total land area. Because they are the earliest known inhabitants of the island, as contrasted to the later colonists, they are called aborigines.

How far back can the Taiwan tribal groups be traced? It is a question which still puzzles cultural historians and anthropologists, but all agree they came in migratory waves. Older theory holds that they are connected with Malayo-Polynesian migration through the Philippines in unrecorded times. Linguistic evidence strongly supports this theory.

According to the anthropologist Chen Chi-lu, "In 1291 the Yuan or Mongol reign had tried to conquer Formosa, but not until the Ming dynasty did the Chinese who lived on the opposite side of the strait begin to move to Taiwan."[2] These earlier people, the Hakkas, migrated from the Yellow River Basin on the Plains of Honan.

Even more recent theory by R. Ferrel holds that "Northern Mongoloid people prior to the Han dynasty are seen as ancestors of Sino-Tibetan and Malayo-Polynesians. According to these people groups, there were three major migrations before Christ — the Ataylic, Tsouic, and Paiwanic."[3]

Until these migrations, it is safe to say that the ten

tribal groups roamed, hunted, and fished at will over the whole island, hindered only by intertribal feudings. These ten groups, now known as tribes, are the Taroko, Tayal, Saisett, Tsou, Rukai, Paiwan, Bunun, Ami, Pyuma, and Yami.

Chinese writers of the Ching dynasty have designated the Formosa aborigines in an interesting way which speaks for itself. They were classified as the Sheng-fan (raw savages), Shan-fan (mountain savages), Yeh-fan (wild savages), Shu-fan (domesticated or "ripe" savages), and the Ping-fan (plains savages).

Those aboriginal inhabitants regarded the island as theirs by right of centuries of possession. When the Chinese intruders came and would not respect their rights, but drove them back into the deep mountain recesses, the Chinese with the well-known queue became the hated enemy. The aborigines sought to avenge the wrongs done to their tribes. This avengement supposedly won the approval of the ancestral braves, whose spirits were watching from the hills. The Chinese head with the queue was the most prized trophy. The plains tribes, or ripe savages, were looked upon as traitors by the other tribes. Because of their betrayal, their heads were also of great value.

The open air rack for skulls was a matter of civic pride. A *National Geographic* report in 1920 observed, "With some of the groups the practice is closely bound up with their religious and social life, while with others it is more especially a question of prowess, and the brave who can display the greatest array of skulls is regarded as the greatest hero."[4]

"But why do your people hunt heads? Is it true that a man must procure a head before he can claim a bride?" the reporter asked a young aborigine.[5]

His answer was, "No, it isn't that; but, of course, the women prefer the men that have brought back the most heads. But it's this way: all my people believe that when we die we all must walk up the rainbow to the Land-of-After-Death. At the end of the rainbow the gateman stands, and when we come he will say to us, 'Show me your hand.' And he will look at our hand, and if he finds it clean he will say, 'Go to the right,' and he will kick us into the dark nothingness below; but if he looks at our hand and finds it stained [with blood] he will say, 'You may enter,' and he will allow us to pass within.''[6]

Although the early tribespeople were uncivilized and unconquered, they should not be judged too harshly for their ways. They had their own set of mores and would not tolerate immorality among their people. Rigid standards of marriage were practiced and arranged by middlemen. If the wife was mistreated by her husband or his family, all she had to do was report it to her middleman, and her husband's family would be fined. The fine was assessed by the wife's village chief and was shared by the wife's family, with the whole village providing a feast.

This system of fining was used to enforce a wide variety of laws and taboos. The resultant feasts contributed to the social life and livelihood of the tribespeople. With the civilizing and education brought later by the Japanese, all the old customs and mores were radically removed along with the authority of the village chief. Often the tribesmen reacted viciously to the Japanese conquerors because of the ravaging of their daughters and women by the police and government authorities sent to subdue them.

Wufeng lived during this difficult period. He was one of the few Taiwanese men able to live at peace among the mountain people because he had their interests at heart. Although he lost his head, he made a lasting impression. Someday another peacemaker, from within the tribe, would make an even more lasting impression for Christ.

21

Tribal children grow up in scenic surroundings.

Chapter 3

Chi-oang, the Reconciler

The woman lay in a huddle weeping at the back of the Presbyterian church in Hualien. The year was 1924. Tears flowed through her fingers covering the wide band of tattoo marks which stretched on her cheeks from ear to ear and around her mouth. Her headpiece, wound around her head, was disheveled, and her handwoven dress rumpled and dirty. The leggings covering her sore, cracked feet did not reveal the many miles she had walked for help.

Waterwheel Lee, the pastor, stood by her and gently spoke to her in Japanese. Raising her head from the floor where she lay weeping, she revealed her thin emaciated face, with high cheekbones and tattoo marks that made her barbaric and ferocious looking. Yet her whole body bespoke the lonely spent woman she was at fifty-two.

She responded to his gentle prodding and began to tell her tragic story. The pastor was amazed. Here in front of him sat the woman whose name was well known as Chi-oang, the Reconciler. This little woman was known all over the island as the Reconciler of the mighty Japanese Empire to the most indomitable tribe, the Sediq, to which she belonged.

Could it be that now was the time God would raise up an aboriginal person to carry the gospel to the tribes high up in the mountains? For this, the Presbyterian

Church, nationals and missionaries, had prayed many years. But an old, spent, discouraged woman of fifty-two?

Yes, God had prepared this remarkable woman to save her tribe, first in reconciling her people to the ruling Japanese, and later in reconciling her people to Christ. She was to be given another name, "Mother of the Taiwan Tribes' Church."

Born about 1872, Chi-oang was a young woman when war broke out in 1894 between Japan and China. At the end of the war, China ceded Taiwan to Japan by treaty. The Japanese ruled Taiwan for fifty years until the end of World War II. At first the people of Taiwan put up a bitter fight but soon capitulated under the superior strength of the Japanese. However, the mountain tribes continued to fight, especially the ferocious Sediq tribe in the Taroko Gorge area on the east coast and central mountain range.

Regardless of eight hundred guards and three hundred miles of electrified wire around the mountain areas, resistance was fierce. The mountaineers learned to fell trees over the fence and were able to smuggle in gunpowder for their guns left by the Dutch. More than seven thousand Japanese and Taiwanese were killed during this period of pacification.

Whenever a village or clan was pacified, the Japanese set up a school and police posts in order to maintain control over the people. Japanese language and culture were imposed on the people along with the state religion of Shintoism. Shrines were built in every village. One by one the tribes submitted. But even with tight control and government authority, the practice of head-hunting was not stamped out.

When Chi-oang was twenty-five her fellow tribesmen bartered her to a Taiwanese man for rifles. A few years later, her Sediq tribal sweetheart murdered her husband. By then she had learned two languages be-

24

sides her own Sediq tongue, Japanese and Taiwanese. She had absorbed the Taiwanese culture and had a taste for the softer living on the plains. After marrying another Taiwanese man, she traveled with him and settled on the prosperous east coast plain.

In 1907 the Japanese searched for someone to help bring peace to the last resisting tribe, Chi-oang's own Sediq tribe. Seeing her people's resistance and knowing that it would mean ultimate extermination if they did not give in, she agreed to help reconcile them to the Japanese rulers. At thirty-six, she used her understanding of the cultures and languages to convince her people. She acted as interpreter for the authorities. She was successful and became known as the Reconciler wherever she went.

With gratitude, the Japanese gave her land and jewelry. She opened a trading post, which she managed successfully until her husband stole everything she had and abandoned her. Old, sick, and worn out, she showed up in the Presbyterian Church in Hualien, an east coast town, seeking help.

How eagerly she listened and responded to Pastor Lee's message of hope and salvation. She accepted Christ and was baptized. She never missed a Sunday to receive instruction in the faith.

A few years later in 1929 when Canadian Presbyterian missionary James Dickson came to Hualien, he was greeted by a joyful, frail woman who wanted to return with him to Tamsui and enter Bible school. Knowing that she would be out of place in a Chinese Bible school, an old woman with tattoo marks from a savage background, yet obviously aglow with the love of God, the leaders of the church pondered what they should do. They reasoned: if a Taiwanese or foreign missionary could not secure mountain permits to enter the aboriginal areas and penetrate the electrified wire barrier, why couldn't a tribal Christian carry the message?

25

So Chi-oang returned with James Dickson and entered the two-year program in Tamsui. She studied hard and learned well. Sent by the Women's Missionary Society of the Hualien Presbyterian Church, she returned there as a missionary to her tribe. She began to teach individuals and groups in the Tayal villages. At first she was not required by the Japanese to have a mountain permit and moved with freedom. But they soon discovered that the threat of Christianity had come to the mountains which they had tried so hard to convert to Shintoism.

The Chinese were allowed to have their own churches, but not the tribal people. When the Japanese discovered that her teaching and preaching were successful, they forbade owning Bibles, meeting in groups, and preaching. People were coming to Christ in large numbers as the government clamped down on her movements and began to persecute the believers.

It became difficult for Chi-oang to travel, and she was forced to move from place to place at night, carried on the backs of believers. The meetings were held outside the villages at night in secret places. An example of God's protection and care for Chi-oang, as His plan for the gospel was fulfilled, can be told by a story of one of her journeys to visit believers.

The Japanese knew that she had left her home. They were on the alert for the old woman as she set out traveling with a group of aborigines, destination unknown. They knew she was conducting secret meetings and were determined to catch her at any cost. Suddenly during one of the meetings the bugle sounded calling the home guard. The atmosphere of prayer, which characterized the rendezvous of the Christians, was broken.

Quickly, two men lifted the frail Chi-oang on their shoulders and fled to the hills. Scouts were sent ahead to the next village, and some remained behind to bring up a rear guard. The Japanese were outwitted, and Chi-oang arrived safely at a village where thirty-four families who had become Christians were waiting to welcome her. But here, too, the guards were on the alert; and soon she had to move on, still being carried, by turns, on the strapping young mountain men's shoulders. Arriving at the next village, Chi-oang's group discovered that the police had already begun a house search.

Hurriedly they decided to stow her away on the train which ran through that coastal village and send her back home. Such a plan was risky, for the Japanese guards had been warned of this possibility. There were three young aboriginal guards, trained by the Japanese, at the train station. They were to arrest her if she came anywhere near the station. Two of the guards, however, were secret Christians; and while the third guard slept, she was given a ticket and smuggled aboard. She hid in the restroom. When she arrived at the next station, six Japanese guards boarded to search for her. But news of her being on the train had traveled faster than the train, and the mountain Christians in that village were prepared for the guards. They boarded the train, bundled Chi-oang up to look like a piece of luggage, and set her on a seat. So she wasn't found at the station; but knowing she was on the train, new guards searched again at the next station. Again failure. Finally, Chi-oang was safe. The loyalty of the Christians, whom she had reconciled to God, protected her until she returned to her village.

After she settled in her home village near Hoelian-kang, leaders of the movement to Christ often came to her. Her home became a place of learning. Many walked all night for twenty miles to spend a few hours with her during the day. Then they walked back the twenty miles to their village to pass on what they had learned. Some stayed, but not for long. For she would send them on their way to make believers in their home villages.

As Christianity spread, the liberty-loving mountain people became gentle in their newfound love of God. They realized that the savage custom of the taking of heads and reprisal towards their conquerors was not compatible with the concept of Christianity. The Japanese suppression of tribal customs had left a vacuum not satisfied by the enforced worship of Shinto. Rather, Christianity, based on love, trust, and truth, and fanned by the fires of the Holy Spirit, produced the miracle of "Pentecost in the Hills."

Persecution descended in earnest on the backs of the mountain believers as World War II loomed over Taiwan. The Japanese were afraid that the mountain people would be in sympathy with the Allied forces and assist in an American landing on Taiwan. Believers were imprisoned and Bibles confiscated, except those smuggled in and hidden under rocks, trees, and in caves. Although many died or suffered permanent injury because of cruel torture, Christians like Weilan Tako became conquerors through tribulation.

Weilan Tako became one of Chi-oang's most remembered converts. He was beaten so severely during the war for his faith that he lost his mind and was kept in a bamboo cage in the middle of the village for a full year. Later he recovered his mind, and, battered and bruised, traveled throughout his tribe, preaching and teaching. An effective lay evangelist, he carried the gospel to every village in Yilan County.

When the Nationalist government took control of Taiwan after the Japanese surrendered in 1945, Taiwan became a province of the Republic of China. In contrast to the Japanese attitude of containing the tribes, the Nationalist government wanted to assimilate them into the Chinese ethnic groups of the plains. Even though access to mountain areas was difficult, it was

28

now much easier to preach the gospel than during the previous four decades. To secure a mountain permit all one needed was a letter from the church governing body stating the mission, two pictures, and identification. Religious instruction was sufficient purpose to visit the mountain areas. This is still followed today.

Postwar freedom to preach Christianity was responded to by many denominations, and Christ's gospel spread rapidly in the mountains and on the plains. Far-sighted James Dickson, a pioneer Presbyterian missionary, in the early postwar period called for Bible translators to get the Word of God into the tribal languages. Today the tribes have Bibles in their own languages, thanks to committed and cooperative efforts of many missionaries and churches.

What of Chi-oang? When she died in the spring of 1946, she had lived to see the Christians, who had suffered so much, free to build places of worship. After her death, a beautiful stone church with a white wooden cross overlooking the Taroko Gorge was erected in her memory. It stands beside the cave where she met with believers during the persecution. The story of Chi-oang, the Reconciler, Mother of the Taiwan Tribes' Church, has become one of the most amazing miracle stories in modern missionary history. Since her time, many mountain people have been raised up by God to take the gospel to their own people.

A woman trained by Chi-oang continues the witness. Her tribal markings are the same as Chi-oang's.

Chapter 4

Tsaopu Village

A river runs through the center of the mountain village of Tsaopu in southern Taiwan. During the summer, torrential rains and typhoon winds slash relentlessly through the mountain pass. The river becomes a swollen gorge of frothy whitewater, beating and rushing its way to the sea ten miles below. Most of the time the river runs quietly, allowing the sounds of the forest birds, cicada, and playing children to echo between the cliffs rising from its sides. Topping the cliffs is a road, and sloping up the sides of the valley are the nestling places of the mountain houses. Beyond, the slopes become steeper mountains, often shrouded with clouds and silvery mists. Verdant greens clothe the mountainsides, broken only by occasional splashes of rhododendron and flowering hibiscus. Trailing bougainvillea give more variation of color.

Following the river is a road known as the South Cross-Island Highway. The natural division in the mountains has made road construction much easier here than farther north. There, the passes reach twelve thousand feet. Here, about twenty-five miles from the tip of the island, the river has made a natural trail for man to follow — first with a walking path, followed by a narrow dirt road, and now by black asphalt. Hugging the mountainside of the road, highway buses, lumber trucks, cars, and unending lines of other vehicular traffic rush along the narrow cliff road with surprising speed.

Most who pass by Tsaopu are completely unaware of what goes on in this little village. Farmers rise with the first gleam of dawn on the distant ridge. They leave the village quietly with tools and a sack of food, traveling on foot over the mountain trails to their fields. Schoolchildren clambering down the trails cross the road to the school, where they pour over books for nine hours of learning. Mothers rising early with their husbands often do their family wash in the river before joining the men in the fields for several hours of work. Old folks, following their own pursuits, watch the goats, dig for sweet potatoes, or help with construction of the narrow terraced fields. Often too old to hobble to the fields, they stay home to watch babies. However, few babies are found at home. Most are tied to their mothers' backs as they work the fields, or the babies may swing in a basket-and-cloth hammock from a nearby tree.

The people of Tsaopu belong to the Paiwan tribe, the second largest of the tribal groups. Scattered along the lower mountain foothills and slopes on the southern half of Taiwan's eastern coast, they live in villages from which they farm higher in the mountains.

The village of Tsaopu was not always in its scenic spot at the head of the gorge, where small mountain streams become the larger river rushing to the ocean. John Hsieh, the first Free Methodist pastor from this village, remembers the move from the inner mountain recesses when he was a lad of ten. He remembers the head shelf in the center of the old village, several hours' hike from the present site. He remembers the fears of the darkness, the places where one never dared go because of lurking evil spirits.

He also remembers the day a tall woman with ramrod posture came to his village in the summer of 1955.

32

She walked with a determined step, with no signs of fatigue from the many years of missionary service behind her. He remembers the wispy hair, always springing out from her net. The color of her hair and eyes were a cause for amazement, especially her eyes. They could be a piercing blue, suddenly changing to a soft melting blue when moved by something she saw that struck the tender place in her spirit. Her name was Alice Taylor, Mrs. James Hudson Taylor II. She came with a handbag and a roll of Sunday school posters. She had traveled by bus from the city of Kaohsiung four hours north and west of Tsaopu.

Accompanying her were two interpreters, a Taiwanese man named Paul Huang who spoke fluent Japanese, and a mountain woman named Mrs. Wang who spoke Japanese and the Paiwan dialect.

John Hsieh was nineteen at the time. He remembers how he knew the message she preached was the one that would really help his people. He had heard about Christ and had believed in Him for salvation in his younger teen years, while attending a Presbyterian church for mountain people in the city of Pingtung. At that time he was a middle school student. Later he returned to Tsaopu, hoping to see his people believe the God he now knew. He wanted them to be set free from their fears, but they did not accept the message.

"Then Teacher-Mother Taylor came," he said, "and I longed for my people to believe. She preached with such love, making the story so simple, and the time was so right for our village to turn to Jesus Christ. Even though I knew my father would be angry at me for inviting her to our house, I did so." Thus she spent the first night in John's mountain home. With a wick in an oilcan hanging from the ceiling and the help of a flashlight, the guest from the outside world told the story of salvation in this Paiwan tribal village of Tsaopu. The house was full of family. The father had also invited his younger brother, the village chief, to come and listen to the strange story the foreigner was telling.

John's uncle's name was Hsieh Chi-chih. By the set of his jaw, one could tell that he was opposed to what was being said. He sat stiffly and listened attentively. He was the headman of the village, well educated, and had served as a provincial legislator. He owned much land and was greatly respected by everyone. He was also addicted to rice wine and other homemade brews made from millet mash. Alcohol was a way of life for many mountain men after their long back-breaking days in the fields. It numbed their senses, and also their fear of the future and unknown. Lurking spirits were held in obeisance by rice and millet wine.

The people in that little mountain home looked from Alice Taylor to their leader Mr. Hsieh to see his reaction. They welcomed her and listened, but gave little response. The next week Alice Taylor returned, bringing again the message of love and release from fears. She came the next week, and the next.

Eventually John's father accepted Christ. How happy John was to have another family member believe. Now he could ask his father for permission to go to Kaohsiung with Alice Taylor, and attend a short-term study of the Bible. Eleven other young men were also invited to attend the classes. Some of them knew little of the gospel, but during the first three or four days they sought and found the Lord. They were taught the fundamentals of Christianity — Bible study, prayer, personal work, and giving. After three weeks, these young men had absorbed all they could, and were sent back to their villages to share Christ.

Two of the young men, one of whom was John, had a better command of the Mandarin language and remained behind. Here was an opportunity to have songs, choruses, and Bible verses explaining the plan of salvation translated into the Paiwan dialect. Singing was a great part of their culture, and songs telling of God's love could easily be sung to their tunes, which were hundreds of years old. John had enthusiasm and an earnest desire to serve the Lord. He was a good student, and it was decided that he should enroll in Holy Light Bible School (now Holy Light Theological College) in Kaohsiung.

By this time Alice Taylor had been coming to Tsaopu for weeks. She came with students from Holy Light to help her. Children were attracted by the sounds of her drum as she walked with the students through the village, singing. The largest courtyard in the village belonged to Mrs. Li. Similar in age and demeanor to Alice Taylor, she felt a peculiar attraction to the foreign lady, and told her that although she did not believe yet, she would welcome the group to use her courtyard. It had a view of the whole village on either side of the gorge, high over the river. The sound of singing and preaching coming over the battery operated public address system carried into every home and courtyard.

The courtyard was large enough for day meetings; but at night when darkness came and the mountain mists descended on them, the people became afraid. They wanted to return to their homes, board up the windows, and keep the spirits away.

John's uncle, Mr. Hsieh, was still adamant against Christianity. He wanted to hang on to the old ways, but kept watching and observing. Because he had the largest house in the village, he invited the foreign guests to sleep in his home. Here he could watch them and see if the story they told coincided with the way they lived.

In time John's father had a plan. He would gather the young people together to go to the mountainsides. In the forest they would cut grass and bamboo for building a house in which to worship the newly found

35

God who had brought them so much peace.

Early one morning he and thirty young people set off with their mountain knives, prepared for a full day's work. They arrived on the hillside where there was just the right kind of grass for the roof. As they worked, they sang the songs taught them by John, and quoted memorized scripture in Mandarin.

Suddenly, the spirit of the day was broken by an angry man running up the hillside towards them, brandishing his mountain knife.

"All work must stop!" he shouted. "We are not going to build a church for the foreign God in this village!" It was Mr. Hsieh, John's uncle. All were terror stricken. He was the greatly respected village elder, headman, and legislator. Now he was using his authority, forbidding a church to be built. Should they listen to him, or to his older brother, John's father? Everyone had observed John's and his father's lack of fear of spirits and darkness, and the new great love they had for everyone in the village since they became Christians. To whom should they listen? The consensus was to listen to the stronger voice of authority.

Yet an even stronger voice spoke through John's father as he began to reason with his brother. He spoke quietly in contrast to the harsh, demanding voice that had been directed at him a few minutes before.

"Can you not see that this new God we have found is not a God to be feared, but a God of love? Can you not see the change in our lives? After all, isn't any belief better than one that fears spirits and devils in rocks and bones and darkness? Can you not see that we are no longer afraid? How can you oppose something that is good for our people? You are a leader and should be happy when someone comes to help us," he reasoned with his brother.

After a long silence Mr. Hsieh dropped his knife.

"All right," he said, "I will not oppose your building

this church. Just do not let it get out of hand. And don't expect me to believe in this God you believe in." With that he stalked down the path to the village.

The young people began singing again and in several hours had completed their work. Their footsteps, in spite of their heavy loads, were light and confident as they returned to Tsaopu. Without the opposition of their village leader, they felt a lot better about building a worship place for their newfound God.

A large area with a grove of betel nut trees was found to be the best location for the new church. Many of the converts had been addicted to betel nut. Chewing this nut gave a narcotic effect, becoming a difficult habit to break. As soon as people were saved, the harmful effects of drinking, smoking, and betel nut chewing were taught, as well as the fact that the Christian's body is the temple of God.

Since betel nut was not chewed after conversion, it was natural to cut these trees down and use them for the framework of the church. Bamboo poles were brought for rafters, and long bamboo strips were used to belt down the mountain grass thatch covering the roof and sides of the building. Poles were tied together with long strands of tree bark. There was not a nail in the structure, and the only expense was for the bolt on the front door. The platform was made of stones cemented together with mud; the rest of the floor was dirt. When the strong winds blew through the gorge, woven bamboo shutters were tied down over the open spaces left for windows. A wooden cross over the front gave the church a distinguished look. For benches, the people brought their own seats and stools.

The first night services were held in the new church, the village people packed in. Songs were sung in their own Paiwan dialect, and it seemed that each one wanted to outdo the other by singing louder. The message of salvation was preached in Mandarin and translated into Paiwanese. Many believed in Christ for salvation that night.

John Hsieh enrolled as a full-time student at Holy Light Theological College. After studying during the week, he would return to his village on weekends, eager to pass on what he had learned. Children's meetings and young people's services, as well as Sunday morning worship, were conducted by the young evangelist. After lunch on Sunday, he set out to other villages located along the river, preaching in three or four each time. Often Alice Taylor would accompany him, teaching, and giving counsel.

Before long there were about twenty believers; however, Mr. Hsieh, the uncle of John, was still a nonbeliever. He was willing to have the foreign guests in his home, and he gladly had his wife cook for them. He listened politely but would have nothing to do with Christianity, choosing rather to lose himself and life's reality in drink.

As the little bamboo church with the grass roof gained in numbers, classes for instruction in Christian baptism and church membership were held. Many of the youth wanted to be baptized, but for this first time, it was decided to baptize only those who were over twenty-five years of age. Twelve men and women responded, and the date was set for March 17, 1957. Everyone prayed for warm weather, but when the day arrived it was cold and rainy. The temperature was fifty-one degrees. The missionary suggested that they wait for warmer weather since they were to be immersed in the river, but no one wanted to wait.

Mrs. Li had also accepted Christ by this time. Somehow she had been overlooked when the candidates were approved for baptism. She came just before the service asking to be baptized.

"Are you sure you're saved?" she was asked by Alice Taylor. Earnestly, she replied, "I certainly am."

"Have you stopped chewing betel nut?" She replied by showing two rows of almost perfectly white teeth.

When the service finally started, the sun was shining brightly and the wind had subsided. As Mrs. Li stepped out of the river, the smile of heaven was on her face.

The village along the river had become alive, alive with new life in Christ which had penetrated the hearts of these Paiwan tribal people.

Young John Hsieh and bride.

Alice Taylor and mothers wash clothes at the river.

Intrepid Teacher-Mother Taylor travels with a mountain Christian.

Chapter 5

The Miracle Church

Early in the history of the Paiwan Free Methodist mountain work, the Tsaopu church became known as the Miracle Church, not only because of the earnestness of the Christians in their desires to have a beautiful place of worship, but also because of God's grace in changing lives from darkness and fear, to faith and hope.

The small grass-roofed church, built in 1957, soon was barely adequate. It was cold and drafty, and the rain came through the roof. The people coming to worship became the butt of village jokes. Undaunted, they continued to worship nightly in their church. One needed to arrive well ahead of time to get a place to sit. Singing and praying was the main form of worship when there wasn't a preacher. After a young Holy Light Chinese graduate named Mr. Li went there to pastor, the congregation began to speak about building a new church.

There were two men in particular who made fun of the Tsaopu believers. They said they would be glad if all the believers in the village died and went to heaven because all the land and property of the believers would be left to them. Liquor had a firm hold on many lives, including these men. Their nights were filled with ribald carousing, in contrast to the joyful singing of the little group of believers in the grass-roofed church.

One day these two men went to the mountains to cut wood. At noon they stopped to rest. As they were resting in the shelter of the cliff, two large rocks rolled off the top of the cliff. One man was pinned under a rock and killed instantly.

One of the greatest fears of animistic people is violent death. Believing that devils and spirits lurk around the body of one killed violently, no one dared to go and bring the body back. The people attending the little bamboo church, however, saw nothing fearsome about going to fetch the body. The Christians lovingly brought the body back and immediately buried it.

That night seventy people crammed into the small church, including the village chief, Mr. Hsieh. He knelt at the crude wooden altar, confessed his sins, and was saved. From that day on, he was released from the power of drink. He exhorted his whole clan to believe. In a short time there were more than one hundred believers, and it became necessary to build a better structure for worship.

The believers went out again into the forest to cut wood. In 1958, the second Tsaopu church was constructed around the first, for the believers did not want to be even one Lord's day without a place to worship. The second church was much larger and consisted of wooden walls and a tin roof, supported by heavy teak beams. When the new outer walls were finished, the old church inside was removed.

The Tsaopu church is a spirit-filled church — filled with the Spirit of God. From the beginning the believers embraced the spiritual gifts, including healing. A man with a club foot walked normally after prayer for him. Children suffering with pneumonia and flu became well after prayer. One young mother's eighteen-month-old child was dismissed from a city hospital with irreversible pneumonia. The mother was told to take her baby home to die. Sadly, with the baby held next to her bosom, she boarded a bus for the three-hour trip back to Tsoapu. On the way, she felt against her heart the breath of life leaving her baby's body. She dared not say anything for fear of being removed from the bus; rather she clutched her dead child to her until she arrived home. In the village the mourners turned out to join the mother in her grief. The sound was heard in the nearby home of Mr. Hsieh. Alice Taylor had already arrived for the weekend meetings and was gathered with the believers for prayer. She and many others came to pray for the baby girl, and God heard their prayers. The baby became warm and began to breathe. After this many more were added to the believers.

Witch doctors practicing witchcraft are now nonexistent in Tsaopu. Many stories are told of their dramatic conversions. One would often throw a piece of carved wood, which she used as a charm, outside the house she wished to harm. She became ill with tuberculosis and was near death. Hearing how Jesus was healing people, she came panting up the hill and asked for prayer. "Are you willing to destroy your charms and forsake that way forever?" she was asked.

"I threw away my charms on the way up here today," she replied. Then she knelt down and prayed for salvation.

Another witch doctor, well known in Tsaopu for her success in witchcraft, had several sons who became Christians. Because of the change she saw in her children's lives, she also believed in Christ for salvation. Many meaningful services were held during which the charms of the witch doctors were burned. These acts signified a complete change from the old life of fear and superstition.

The pattern for worship in the Tsaopu church is beautiful. Front seats are always filled first, often an hour in advance of the service. Men sit on one side and women on the other. Singing and united prayer are an important part of worship. In the early years when the church was small and there was not enough room, the people were packed in with many standing at the back and at open windows. Once a month there is an all-night prayer meeting. Every night of the week all over Tsaopu, voices can be heard in worship to God, either in the sanctuary or in home cottage meetings. There is a strong youth choir which ministers all over the district and assists in evangelism.

Tsaopu has set a pattern for church building which the other Paiwan churches have followed. Under Peter Wu's ministry the church underwent its third building program. Strong laymen, like Mr. Hsieh, led the way for financing the new church. He sold twenty acres of prime timber land. Nine-tenths he gave for building the new church, and one-tenth he kept for himself. As in the previous structures, the new church was built around the old; and when it was completed the inside walls were removed.

The new church was adequate in size, holding up to three hundred people. The walls and floors were cement, the aisle and altar of hand-polished terrazzo. The tin roof was supported by large beams, and glass windows provided good ventilation. It was dedicated in 1960 with the words "Holiness unto the Lord" engraved on the wall behind the altar. Already the first phase of the next building program has begun, for the tin roof has been replaced with a cement slab that will become the floor for the fourth sanctuary.

The church has also set the pattern for self-support of the pastors. Giving is stressed — not necessarily monetary gifts, for money the mountain people have little of — but a tenth of what they grow is given. In Sunday morning services there is little cash in the offering bags, but the altar is often piled high with rice, millet, sweet potatoes, and beans. Very often a fowl, whose leg is tied to the communion table, crows in church. Yearly when the harvest is gathered, a special day of thanks to the Lord is set aside. On this day bags and bags of produce are offered at the altar to the Lord. The produce is sold, and the cash immediately used for the work of the church and evangelism.

Pioneering the Paiwan tribal work, and a name almost synonymous with the name Miracle Church, was Alice Taylor, an intrepid missionary with unbounding energy and zeal. Her vision was to see people saved, lives changed, and men called into the ministry to share the gospel with their own people. From the beginning one of the most important aspects of the miracles of the Tsaopu church has been the many called into full-time Christian service.

Soul winning was Teacher-Mother Taylor's consuming passion. If the slightest interest was shown by a seeker in salvation, that was the moment to be saved; and if an individual showed any interest in full-time Christian service, that was the moment to heed the call and begin training for such service to Christ. Young men and women, as a result of her tender shepherding, have been trained at Holy Light. They in turn have led the way for the development of a strong Paiwan mountain church.

Alice Taylor taught all week at Holy Light; then early Saturday morning boarded a bus — sometimes alone, but more often with students — and traveled that dusty, wearisome road for three or four hours, followed by hours of walking to various villages.

Enduring great discomfort, she traveled lightly with just a small handbag. She ate what was prepared, and for the Paiwan people this was often meagre. Millet and sweet potatoes and a few fried greens were the main fare. She lived and slept right with the mountain people in their homes. Often she crawled into a bed with another family member, sometimes sleeping under nets, sometimes not, enduring bugs and rats.

Teacher-Mother Taylor preached in all kinds of weather, under all circumstances. One day as she preached in a church she discovered that she didn't have the attention of the people. Instead, they were gazing over her head. Looking up she discovered that they were absorbed in watching a snake that was making its way along the beam just above her head. Interestingly, one man caught the snake, sold it, and placed the proceeds in the offering.

Many of the churches, which were offshoots from the Tsaopu church, planned their Christmas programs around her schedule. They wanted Teacher-Mother Taylor to be at them. One Christmas she traveled by bus and hiked two miles to the first church. Then she caught another bus and went two miles up a steep trail to the second church for its program.

She was extremely thirsty on arrival, but found the Christians had finished their united meal, and there was not a drop of boiled water left to drink. She preached in that program, then slipped away during the altar service for the third bus ride and hike up another steep trail. How she longed to wet her lips, but dared not if the water was not boiled. As she ate her prepared sandwich and waited for the bus, she saw some young people nearby eating freshly pulled turnips. How her mouth watered for those turnips. Finally she was able to procure a turnip from the young people in exchange for some hard candy she had in her pocket. Peeling back the skins with her fingers, she quenched her thirst; then she got on the bus and proceeded to her next meeting.

Early in the Paiwan work, Alice Taylor and others, concerned that the dialect be reduced to writing, worked many months to produce a Paiwan hymnbook. John Whitehorn, an English Presbyterian missionary, worked for years along with a young Paiwan evangelist to reduce the Scriptures to phonetic script. Although the Japanese Bible was in use in the tribe, only those old enough to have received education under the Japanese could understand it. Today, primarily Chinese Mandarin Bibles are used in worship services, with the pastor giving a free translation into the local dialect. Because Mandarin is taught in all the public schools, most of the tribal people under the age of fifty understand Mandarin Chinese. However, all the preaching is done in the local tribal dialect, which is still the medium for communication. The early hymnbook is still used, but since then native lyric tunes, hundreds of years old, have had Christian words put to them, and are frequently heard in the worship services.

Long since Teacher-Mother Taylor has retired, the Tsaopu church remains the center for evangelism from which new churches are started. Weekly Theological Education by Extension programs are held there for leading laymen and pastors from surrounding Paiwan villages. Professors from Holy Light in Kaohsiung come to hold the classes. Laymen and lay pastors in turn go back to their villages, forming strong leadership in the Paiwan Free Methodist churches, which have become a district in the Annual Conference of the Taiwan Free Methodist Church.

Since those days when Holy Light students and Alice Taylor came on weekends to evangelize, the Tsaopu church had had four pastors. Presently, John Hsieh, the first strong Christian and student worker in Tsaopu, is pastoring. He heads the present building program. The Tsaopu Free Methodist Church is still a place where lives are being transformed to the glory of God.

Alice Taylor and church leaders gather in front of the early grass church at Tsaopu.

A bountiful produce offering is given at the Tsaopu Miracle Church.

A vibrant congregation rejoices in front of the third Tsaopu church. Missionary James H. Taylor III is in the center.

Chapter 6

Paul and Lydia

Late in the year 1957, God touched Paul Kuo, a lad of fifteen in the village of Tsaopu. Like John Hsieh, Paul was born in the old village site of Tsaopu high in the interior mountains. His father was a farmer, growing sweet potatoes, millet, and dry rice. As most of their food was taken by the war effort, Paul grew up hungry most of the time. When he was five, the old village was moved to the new site, and he was given the opportunity to attend the village school until he was eleven years old. Because they were so poor, Paul had no chance to continue his education on the plains as others his age did.

His father sent him off to the nearby village of Danlu to work in a government middle school as a cleaning and messenger boy. After a short time a school clock disappeared, and Paul was blamed and dismissed. In shame he returned to his village.

Soon he again left home for the village at the base of the mountains, where the river joins the sea. In the village of Fengkang he worked as a water buffalo herder for a wealthy farmer. He had a carefree life, learning to ride and race the water buffalo. One day Paul allowed the buffalo to get into the wrong field, and they totally plundered it with their hoofs and ate the crops. He was severely beaten for his mistake and sent back to his village.

Hurt and depressed, he worked in his father's fields in the mountains around Tsaopu. He had few friends and felt that all of life's joys had deserted him. One by one his friends had either gone on with their education or were working in nearby cities. Both he had proven he could not do with success.

One afternoon he heard the sound of singing across the valley. Being a shy boy and already smitten with little self worth, he dared not go close to where he saw a group of strangers. He hid behind a bush across the valley where he could see the courtyard of Mrs. Li. A tall foreign lady and Chinese young people were singing loudly. Through a megaphone the words came clearly: "This world is not my home . . . heaven is . . ." No one called him to come; indeed, no one saw him hiding behind the bush.

Each week the group returned and he was there to listen. But each week he hid behind a bush a little closer to the sound of the singing. During the week, he sang the songs he had heard as he worked in the fields and thought about the words that had been spoken — strange but comforting words to his sore battered heart. The strangers had talked about a man named Jesus who they said was the Son of God. Jesus had suffered so that they would not need to suffer anymore.

Eventually Paul arrived at the courtyard. He still used a bush for cover. It had taken him six months, and when he arrived and the invitation was given to accept Christ as Savior, Paul appeared. John Hsieh, four years older than Paul, helped him pray through to peace with God.

Experiencing God's love gave new courage and esteem to Paul. He still worked in his father's fields, but now he sang with the confidence and happiness that salvation brings. He could hardly wait for the group to come from Holy Light on weekends, so that he could learn more about Christ. Under the tutelage of John

Hsieh, Paul became a leader among the young people. He was with them that day on the mountain when John's uncle, Mr. Hsieh, brandished the mountain knife, trying to force the work to stop.

As Paul grew and matured, he began to feel a desire to serve the Lord as a full-time pastor to his people. Everything he learned from the visiting Holy Light students and missionaries, he used in his Sunday school teaching. But he was shy and still feeling some personal inadequacies, especially in the use of Mandarin. Having had little opportunity to attend school and to learn Mandarin, Paul was sure he would not qualify for Holy Light. So he quietly made plans to study in another school for mountain people on Taiwan's eastern coast.

Packing his bags on Saturday, he went to the church to say farewell to the young people. Whom should he meet but Alice Taylor. She was surprised at his plans, and said she would take him back with her the next day to Kaohsiung. He would be tested, and then they would decide the best plan for him to follow for his training for the ministry.

After testing, Paul was able to enter the three-year Bible training program. At first it was hard for him to comprehend the difficult Mandarin characters; but because of his love for the Lord and his sincere desire to serve Him, he did well.

Like John Hsieh, Paul also traveled back to his tribal village of Tsaopu and to other villages in the low foothills of the mountains on weekends. There were several villages along the river where Tsaopu was located. Here there was no gospel witness and people were hungry for salvation.

"I would often preach six times in a weekend," he said, "always using and repeating what my Bible professors taught me during the week, especially Teacher-Mother Taylor's lessons. God blessed me, and

I saw many of my people saved while I was still in school." Several mountain young people, among them the son of the village leader, Mr. Hsieh, were called into the ministry through Paul's leadership.

Because all young men in Taiwan must serve in the military for two years, Paul's study at Holy Light was interrupted. But God's plan for his life was still being fulfilled, even when he was in full-time military service.

Back in Tsaopu there was a beautiful young lady named Lydia. She and Paul had played together as children and been classmates in school. As they grew up, love developed between them. When separated, they continued their friendship by writing, and their romance blossomed. However, Paul didn't dare to think they could possibly marry.

The Paiwan tribe has a matriarchal system. The eldest daughter inherits the land. Her family name is also assumed by the man she marries. Her social status is high. Lydia, a high school graduate, was the oldest daughter in her wealthy family, and for years her parents made plans for her to marry her equal socially.

One day while Paul was in the military, he received a desperate letter from Lydia telling that she was being forced to marry a man she didn't love, a man who was well known, of high social standing, and wealthy. He was much older than she, and a heavy drinker. Paul, too, became desperate, wanting to help her but knowing there was little he could do to stop the marriage. Both families had been planning this for many years, and would not allow any outside interference. As her desperate letters continued to arrive, Paul wrote to his family begging them to intercede for him, but their reply was to forget her and look for another girl.

In desperation Paul took the packet of letters from Lydia to his superior officer. He was given three days leave to return home to Tsaopu to do what he could. But three days were not enough, and on the last afternoon he received a message from her that she was running away.

She planned to use her grandmother as a ruse and take her on the bus to Fengkang, the town where the mountains meet the sea. Then Lydia would put her grandmother on a return bus for home. Would Paul also come to Fengkang so they could discuss what they should do, away from the confines of the village where there were eyes and ears everywhere? For her to do this took great courage. This was not the way of the mountain social system.

When Grandmother was back on the bus headed for home, Paul appeared. What could he do with Lydia? He knew that he would be blamed for her precipitous dash to freedom. To marry her, as his heart told him to do, would alienate him forever from his own people.

Christianity had not yet broken down all the age-old customs pertaining to arranged marriages. His leave was up and he dared not risk trouble with his army commanders. Suddenly his thoughts turned to Teacher-Mother Taylor, who seemed so wise in many ways. She had been his mentor in spiritual growth; why not in things of the heart? So boarding a bus for Kaohsiung, three hours to the north, the two young people arrived at her doorstep late in the afternoon.

The Taylors were not unaware of their romantic involvement and ached with them for their problem. As they all prayed together and sought God's will, Alice Taylor thought of a possible solution. She would seek the help of the National Women's Organization concerned with women's rights. After the whole situation was explained to them, the women of the organization were happy to send a delegation to Tsaopu to meet with both families, settle the dispute, and prevent a forced marriage. Lydia stayed with the Taylors until she could enter Holy Light, and with great relief Paul returned to his military post. The elders of the village were angry with him for interfering in their affairs, and immediately fined him 500 New Taiwan dollars ($12.50 U.S.). He didn't have the money to pay, and to this day he has not paid the fine, for later the charges were dropped.

In 1964, Paul and Lydia were graduated in the same class from Holy Light. He went to serve his first pastorate in the village of Danlu — the Paiwan village six miles east on the South Cross-Island Highway. This was the same village where he was so shamefully treated as a young lad in the village school. Lydia returned to her home village of Tsaopu to prepare for marriage.

Eight months later they were married. What a long way Paul had come since a lad of fifteen, bruised and sore in spirit, smitten with poor self-esteem, he had heard for the first time the sweet gospel message from across the valley in Tsaopu. How tenderly he had responded, throwing himself into the Word and learning the Christian life. God had nurtured and prepared him, and Lydia, to lead their people into a beautiful ministry. This ministry would bear fruit for the kingdom among the Paiwan tribal people.

Paul and Lydia Kuo.

Chapter 7

The Haunted House Church

Five days after the wedding of Paul and Lydia, the elders of the Paiwan churches met for a retreat in Fengkang. It was a time of inspiration, evaluation, and planning for the future. The elders decided that new work should be started in the village of Mudan, high up on the central mountain ridge. The following exciting story of the Mudan church as told by Paul will take us back eighteen years to the time when he began his formal ministry with his new bride.

On the first day of the Paiwan elders' retreat, Teacher-Mother Taylor asked me if we would be willing to go to Mudan and start a church. I immediately suggested someone else. The second day of the retreat, she again asked me if we would go, and I again found another person and another excuse . . . such as the building of a new church in Danlu where I was needed. Five days in a row she asked if we would go; and finally I said, "I will go, but I haven't asked my wife yet."

When I asked my wife I was so afraid that she would say no . . . and I didn't want to displease her. After all, getting her was not that easy. But she was happy to go with me; and when I told Teacher-Mother Taylor, tears of joy came to her eyes. She assured us that we would be going with the help of the Holy

Spirit; many would be behind us in prayer and she would come on weekends to help us.

After an anointing service, we were on our way. The village seemed so remote, and the dirt road to Mudan was difficult. With all our things piled high on a three-wheeled motorized jitney, it took three hours of bumping and sliding to get there. We found no Christian witness, in spite of a population of about one thousand. Nor could we find a place to live.

In fact, it took twenty days to find a place for us. No one wanted to rent to outsiders who had the intention of changing village beliefs. Walking through the village one day, we noticed an old broken-down house that appeared to be abandoned. We inquired for the owner and were informed that the house was haunted, and that we certainly wouldn't want to rent it. It was presently occupied by the spirits of the dead who had died within, and no one dared to enter.

The Tsaopu Christians were supportive of us during these days. When they saw the house, they fearlessly walked inside. It was dirty and full of cobwebs. The windows were all broken, and the floor uneven and pitted. However, the supporting structure was strong, and the house had lots of possibilities. Finally, a bargain was struck with the owners next door to buy it for eighty dollars. I quickly wrote to Teacher-Mother Taylor. She felt that it was such a reasonable price we must get it immediately.

The Christian brothers and sisters from Tsaopu remained until it was cleaned, painted, and repaired. All this time the village people walked by at a distance, thinking we were crazy to consider such a place for any purpose.

Hadn't we heard that two people had committed suicide by drinking insecticide in that house? Also, the village drunk had fallen into the drainage ditch by the house, and had died a violent death. Not to mention that a dog had bitten someone who had crawled into the house to die — four violent deaths, and all their spirits left lurking.

Now this building was not only to be the church, but also our dwelling place. An inside partition was built, and behind that was our bed, a desk, and a small table. Our kitchen was a lean-to against the back wall, with no walls to keep out the rain and wind, just a roof. We had a cooking pot between three stones.

Most of the house was the church with a pulpit and several benches. We also had a blackboard, and later we got a small pump organ. My wife has a beautiful voice and loves to sing. It gave her great comfort to sit and sing for many hours. I am sure the villagers listened to her singing long before they listened to my preaching.

I was not afraid, but I must tell the truth. My wife was terrified. There was no electricity, so we had to put a wick in an oilcan hanging by a wire from the ceiling. We let it burn all night. There wasn't much light, and the many shadows on the wall struck terror to my wife's heart. Whenever I went out at night, she always accompanied me. She refused to stay alone.

One night she woke up screaming with terror. I quickly started to light a candle, but she restrained me. In the darkness she lay in my arms trembling. She told me that on the shelf opposite where we were sleeping, she saw a figure of someone. At first she thought it was a devil or a spirit of the dead that had died in the house. But soon she became quiet and calm. She said a warm peace spread over her body, and she realized that it wasn't a devil, but the Lord himself on that shelf. I could see nothing; but as God revealed himself to her in that moment, her fears melted away. She was never again afraid to be alone in that house, day or night.

When the church was ready for people to come and hear the gospel, no one came. Night after night we used our drums to call the people to worship, but we could not get anyone to enter the church. So we walked around the village, preaching as we beat on the drum. Not only were the people afraid to enter the church because of the spirits, but they wouldn't let us enter their homes because we might have the spirits on our bodies. Often our fellow Christians from Tsaopu came to encourage us. And we could count on Teacher-Mother Taylor to be there on weekends for support and encouragement.

After a month of the people watching us, a well respected witch doctor accosted us on the street and said, "Teacher, you are still living in that house and nothing has happened to you?"

"Nothing," I said.

"Well, before, even during the daylight hours we could see spirits and devils in that house. Now we don't see them anymore," she said.

My reply was, "If I didn't believe in a God greater than the devils you say are in that house, then I couldn't live there either."

"How do you explain that?" she asked.

"You are the greatest witch doctor in all this area, with the greatest powers. I challenge you to come and sleep in our house for one night. Let's see if the spirits you worship are strong enough to protect you." But she wasn't willing to accept the challenge. However, she did tell people that we couldn't be that bad, that in fact we were very brave to be living in that house. Soon young people and children began to come to services, but not adults.

I became friendly with the local farmers by going out and working with them on their crops. I had their respect, but they still wouldn't listen to the words of the gospel. We knew that some miracle had to take place to break through the barriers of superstition and fear.

One evening we felt led by God to go to a certain

58

home where my wife had been helping with the care of the children of a sick mother. She had twin boys and a little girl. Her husband was a retired policeman. The wife had been ill for over three years, and bedfast most of that time. All of her husband's money had been used for doctor bills. She could eat very little, and felt that she was going to die at any time. As we entered the home, we sensed that God was with us. I explained to Mrs. Huang that we had come in the name of the Lord Jesus to pray for her healing, but first she must repent of her sins and believe in Jesus Christ as her Savior. She looked at me, and then at my wife and said, "I am willing." My wife and I knelt by her straw mat and helped her pray the sinner's prayer of repentance. Then putting my hands on her, we prayed for her healing. We left that small house jubilant, so jubilant that the tears were running down both our faces. This was our first believer.

Early the next morning we were sent a message to come to Mrs. Huang's home. When we arrived there, she was doing her housework. She had eaten a large breakfast, and was singing.

"After you left last night I felt a hot burning in my stomach, and my body felt light. Now I have eaten a good meal for the first time in years, and I feel like working. I am healed by God," she stated. Mrs. Huang immediately began to testify to all her friends, and to those who didn't know anything about God.

Because the whole village knew of her weak physical state, in fact had expected her to die at any time, they were amazed. Her husband and his entire family believed, and this couple became our closest helpers in the work. Everything they had they divided with us. Half of their millet and rice crop was given to the church. Every morning at 4:30 they came to our door, entered the church, and we prayed together. After this miracle, people began to get saved and our little church began to grow.

59

About this time another miracle happened to a woman named Mrs. Lin. She was the daughter of the village headman. She had a nervous disorder, and like Mrs. Huang had spent most of the family money on psychiatrists and doctors, even traveling as far as Kaohsiung to seek help. Everyone feared her, especially her children. She carried her baby around by the hair on his head, and the whole village worried that something terrible would happen.

Mrs. Huang accompanied my wife and me to the woman's home. My first question was as always: Was she willing to find the Savior who would help her have peace and joy? We told her simply the plan of salvation, and she said she was ready to believe. My wife and I and Mrs. Huang knelt down. Putting our hands on her head and body, we began to pray for healing of her mind. As we prayed her body began to shake and tremble, but we did not stop praying as long as she was shaking. I don't know how long we prayed, but for a long time and with loud voices we beseeched God to heal her. Then gradually she became quiet. As we finished praying, we looked up at her and there was a beautiful expression in her eyes, in contrast to the fear that was there before. That night her husband also became a Christian, and from that day on she didn't need to see doctors and psychiatrists, or buy any more drugs.

Because Mrs. Lin was a headman's daughter, she had many objects which she had used in animistic worship. She gathered them up and we had a burning ceremony for them. We now had two strong couples who were believers. The second couple also joined the early morning prayer meetings at 4:30. We prayed for the salvation of the entire village.

Soon we had another interesting conversion in Mudan. The man's name was Mr. Hung. He owned much land, and even had two trucks which he used to transport goods to and from Mudan. We felt burdened for him and went to his house to preach. He welcomed us, but really felt he was much too busy and successful to have anything to do with our religion. He admitted that it was truly a miracle that we could live in our house unharmed, but he was happy as he was. He just didn't have the time.

Then one day he had a problem, which even the witch doctor could not solve. Each time his sons went to a certain section of his land, they saw spirits. Neighbors went, too, but could see nothing. His sons became terrified to go, but nevertheless had to till the land. They always came back with stories of what the spirits had said to them. Eventually they fell ill after working the land, and could not be persuaded to return to those fields. So the fields lay fallow. Mr. Hung began to feel the pinch financially, as that large section of his land produced nothing. He finally hired the witch doctor to go and communicate with the spirits to find out what the problem was. The witch doctor came back with a message from the spirits that nothing would ever grow on that land, for it belonged to them. Mr. Hung was dismayed. He decided to go and see if there really were devils on the land. Sure enough, he came back terrified and felt ill.

The whole village, of course, knew what was going on. Most of the people were also terrified. Then Mr. Hung began to dream. On three nights in a row he dreamed of heaven, and all its glories and joys. When he tried to enter, he was stopped at the door because of his uncleanness, caused by his sin. A voice said to him, "If you want to enter heaven, you will have to prepare. Go to the house where the American missionary visits, and they will show you the way."

The next day he and his whole family came to our church. He told me the dream, and I knew that God had spoken to him. So I explained the way to get into heaven by repentance and belief in Jesus as Savior. That day five adults and three children were saved.

After we had had a service in his fields, we started to hold meetings in Mr. Hung's home. From that time on, no one saw any more spirits in his fields. These same fields which had yielded nothing for so long began to have bumper crops. From then on, the crops from that part of the land were donated to the Lord.

The eighty-year-old grandmother in this family had not believed. When she became ill with the flu, she sacrificed three pigs to the spirits and witch doctors, but got no better. We explained Christ's love for her, and sentence by sentence she repeated our prayer. At the close of the prayer she said, "How can I pray to the true God when there are articles connected with demon worship concealed in the kitchen? Can you help me remove them?"

In a dark corner of the kitchen, under the table, we found a bamboo hat and a food bowl with the remains of food and betel nuts that were an offering to her husband who had died twelve years previously. All were carefully held in place by three flat stones. As we worked together to remove these stones we sang, "Victory, Victory, Hallelujah."

Nine months after arriving in Mudan we had our first baptism with nine adults. The church grew, and in 1969, we built a new church. Presently Mudan is sending strong laymen to a nearby village where they are holding cottage meetings and praying that there will soon be enough believers to build a church.

Five years after the church was established in Mudan, my wife and I were appointed to another village called Chukeng. God has blessed our ministry. We have built six churches for our people and pastored in seven. Praise the Lord.

Paul and Lydia Kuo stand in front of their Mudan home, the "haunted house church."

Burning pagan worship articles.

63

The growing Mudan congregation.

Chapter 8

To Marry a Blind Man

"Marry a blind man? You can't mean it, Lord!" Standing at the pulpit before Esther Chu was a handsome young seminary student from Holy Light. He had been coming on weekends to her mountain church in Chukeng to fulfill his requirements for practical service. He had witnessed to what God had done for him in his blindness. As she gazed at him, Esther had the inner feeling that this was the man she was to marry.

Beautiful, black-eyed, singing, joyous Esther was the first girl in her Paiwan tribe to graduate from high school. She had spent her early years in the little mountain village of Chukeng, nestled in the foothills of the central mountain range. From her front door was a panoramic view of the sparkling ocean. The mists rising from the sea often hid the mountaintops behind her home. In these mountains, Esther had grown into loveliness as she tended her grandfather's goats and cattle. Early in life, she had accepted Jesus Christ as Savior. Through weekly visits from the young mountain Bible school students in Kaohsiung, a church and Sunday school had been established in her village. She had excelled in school, and her parents had encouraged her education beyond the usual sixth grade level. Her teachers had fostered her natural ability, and had introduced her to a good high school in the nearest city. At the top of her graduating class, she had received a scholarship for medical school.

It seemed, however, that the Lord had other plans for her. Esther had come home to be with her family for a period of time, and now she had a keen interest in this blind man. Perhaps God wanted her to serve Him by being a teacher to the blind. . . .

As Peter Wu preached that morning, instead of letting her eyes linger on the rising mists from the sea, Esther listened to his testimony, fascinated.

He told how as a young mainland Chinese soldier he had aspired, with others in the Chinese Army, to regain mainland China.

Shortly after he entered the army, a battery he was recharging exploded in his face. When he regained consciousness, all the world was in darkness. Darker, though, was the bitterness in his soul. Emerging from the trauma of the accident, he decided to study Braille. The only place to learn was in the home of a missionary, Bessie Cordell. She introduced him to a comforting Christ, and gave him a Braille Bible to read. He soon mastered Braille, but would not accept the teaching of the Book he used. He argued and debated with his teachers and classmates. Gradually, the Holy Spirit began to work in Peter, and he gave his life to Jesus Christ. Soon he felt he could best serve Him by entering the ministry.

In time, Esther timidly approached her missionary friend, James Taylor II, about her feelings of love for Peter. She was encouraged to enter Holy Light and train as a Christian leader.

Esther's family was aghast at what she planned to do with her life. "You're throwing your life away marrying this man. Don't you know you are the most promising girl in the tribe? We will throw ourselves into the ocean if you persist in this terrible plan," they threatened.

But for Peter, the prospect of a beautiful bride who

would overlook his handicap, and see him for himself, brought nothing but amazement at the goodness of God. He had not been unaware of the gentle mountain girl. He had heard her lilting voice in song, heard her soul-searching prayers. He had heard his classmates describe her beauty.

When the proposal was made, how he longed to break traditional customs and touch her face. How he wanted his eyes to see her as they courted.

Esther was strong in her determination to follow God at any cost, and resisted her parents' pressure. While still in seminary, Peter and Esther were married, and she became his eyes and guiding hands. At the same time, she kept up with her own subjects. She became the first woman to graduate from Holy Light with a degree in theology.

Their first assignment after graduation was to pastor the Tsaopu church, where there were now more than one hundred members. It was not an uncommon sight to see Esther playing the organ and directing the choir, then standing up with her husband and interpreting his message into the Paiwan dialect. His blindness did not keep him from ministering in the people's homes. Often, the two could be seen wending their way up and down the sides of the mountain visiting his people. She would be beside him guiding his footsteps. Even with four children and the duties of motherhood, she still found time to guide his feet in his pastoral ministry.

An example of Peter and Esther Wu's love for the Lord, and their evangelistic fervor, can be seen in an exciting event which took place during their ministry in Tsaopu.

One day the Wus boarded a bus at Tsaopu to go to Taitung on the east coast for business. With them they had their seven-year-old son. Soon after they boarded, the bus careened around a narrow curve on the cross-island mountain road. The driver was hurrying to make his next scheduled stop. As he rounded the curve at breakneck speed, he met a large truck head on. Swinging quickly to the edge of the road, he struck a soft shoulder, and the bus plunged over the cliff.

As it fell, Esther was thrown through a window and into the path of the falling bus. She would have been killed if a tree had not stopped the downward plunge of the bus.

An hour or two later, the Wus were being treated in a government hospital in Taitung. He had several fractures, and Esther had head wounds, and was in deep shock.

The bus company assumed all the expenses and urged the family to avail themselves of the best medical assistance, even offering to pay for a private room so that they could be together. Friends who had come from the church urged them to do so for their own comfort.

"Oh, no," they said, "please leave us in the ward. We have so many opportunities here to witness about God's protection and love."

In pain and blindness they remained in the ward for several weeks. They witnessed and sang. Often Peter Wu read his Braille Bible aloud, and Esther translated what he had read into the Paiwan dialect for the benefit of the mountain people in the ward.

Mrs. Chen, a woman from the east coast mountain village of Tuban, was a patient in the ward. Tuban residents have the dubious reputation of consuming more alcohol than any other east coast village. A church had closed its doors there, and the village was without an active Christian witness. Mrs. Chen listened to the testimony of Esther and Peter, and joyfully accepted Christ as Savior. Then her first thought was that her village should have another chance to hear the gospel, so she invited the Wus to come to her village to preach.

After the Wus returned to Tsaopu, they challenged their members to respond to this need of taking the gospel to Tuban. The Tsaopu congregation had completed three major building projects of its own, and had spearheaded other evangelistic efforts in villages to the west, north, and south. Why not go east? Even though Tuban was more than an hour by bus, over narrow mountain roads, Christians from Tsaopu eagerly gathered each week under Peter Wu's leadership for the evangelization of Tuban.

Laymen were in training in the Theological Education by Extension classes in Tsaopu, and were able to put into practice their training as they gathered in Mrs. Chen's home for meetings. Often, the Tsaopu youth choir with Esther directing came to sing and challenge the youth. Not only did Mrs. Chen's family accept Christ, but so did many of her neighbors.

Today Tuban has an organized church with twenty-six members and more than a hundred people, including children, attending the Sunday services. A new church is nearly completed.

The witness of blind Pastor Wu and his consecrated wife, Esther, has been used to bless many people in the mountains. The power of God's Spirit has been evidenced in their lives over the years as they have pastored churches. Many have come to Christ through their witness and radiating love.

Peter and Esther Wu and their family.

Holy Light Theological College student Peter Wu.

Part II

To the Rukai Tribe

Rukai girl babysits her brother wearing tribal headpiece.

Chapter 9

Haucha Village

The mountain village of Haucha is deep in the inner recesses of the south central range of mountains. The people living here belong to the Rukai tribe. Its name Haucha means "good tea," named after the crystal clear, icy mountain pool at the head of the village. Luxuriant, green foliage surrounding the pool dips into the water, except where there is a well-worn path leading to the shallows. There, children play with joyful abandon; mothers wash clothes, ever watchful for the children as the current pulls toward the exit of the pool.

As a small stream, the water pours through a yawning chasm and falls another fifty feet. Then, joined by a thousand rivulets and mountain streams, it rushes on, wearing the rocks bare and eating out the sides of the mountain, until it merges with the mother river a mile below.

Arching the chasm where the stream leaves the pool is a bridge of logs intertwined with vines, which not only hold the logs together, but twist up into a handrail. The bridge heaves and groans with the weight of bodies carrying loads of produce and firewood. Nevertheless, it has withstood the weight of man, wind, and rain for hundreds of years.

The chasm wall is a steep face of rock soaring into the sky, until it tapers to become an eyetooth-shaped crag of mountain. This mountain pinnacle is the village's watching post. On the one side the slate-roofed houses glisten in the morning sun, often blinding the eyes of the guard as he watches the path that leads over the log bridge and out of Haucha.

Three walking hours down the trail lies the village of Maer, and across the valley is Majya; both are Paiwan villages, and once enemies of Haucha. From here the danger often came. The crag served as the doorway and needed to be guarded.

Tradition says that Haucha traces its beginnings to the wandering of a pet bear. A man had a bear who used to wander from home. Searching one day for it, he found the bear sitting beside a beautiful waterfall. At the foot of the fall was a deep, crystal pool. No amount of coaxing could remove the bear from his post. The man, unwilling to part company with his bear, decided he would move his home from deep in the mountains to where the bear was sitting. No one knows when this took place, but gradually other Rukai tribal people found this spot to be ideal with its excellent water source. They came and made their dwellings in Haucha, until with 150 families, it became the second largest village in the district.

Besides being surrounded by protective mountains on three sides, Haucha is set in a panorama of distant mountain ranges, sometimes shrouded in clouds, sometimes hazy from the tropical sun, but most often an ethereally clear melting of multishades of green. Far below in the valley bottom, the river can be seen curving its way through the passes to the sea.

In this remote setting, the village is dug into the side of the mountain and well protected from typhoon winds. The back wall of each slate home faces the side of the mountain, and the roofs of slate slabs are continuous with the courtyard on the next level. The houses are built side by side, and resemble huge stairsteps stacked up against the mountain.

74

Into one of these homes a baby boy was born in the early 1930s. He was destined to grow and change the way of life for his people. Peng Chih-ting was the second child of seven born to the Peng family. Happy, bouncing, energetic, he was one of the children who loved to swim in the natural water pool at the head of the village. Or he loved to accompany his father to the narrow rocky terraced mountainside where millet, sweet potatoes, and corn were grown to sustain the family.

Sometimes he was assigned to herd the family goats in the mountains above the village. The goats' paths crisscrossed, gaining in altitude until the village slate roofs were mere dots below, catching the morning rays of sunshine.

As he climbed with the goats, Peng's mind would wander.

He thought of the fun he could have if he were swimming with his friends, and his bare feet would kick the stones, sending them defiantly over the mountainside to keep rolling into the valley below.

He thought of the bush robins, heard but seldom seen, as they trilled their sweet notes. He listened for the sounds of other birds, and watched their flight patterns as his father had taught him.

He thought of the stories of valor his father had told him, of the fighting men in the village who prepared for battle against Maer and Majya. He knew about their ambush spots. The stories always filled him with dread.

He relived the strategies and helped plan the ambushes, remembering how his father spoke of the heads brought back to the village — Japanese, tribal, and barbarians from across the sea. All were stored in the skull racks.

He thought of his father's hunting prowess, evidenced by the rows of wild boar jaws lining one wall of the family home. No longer were human heads taken; instead, the boar jaws were proudly displayed.

Peng also thought of the changes which had come during his short lifetime to his family, village, and tribe.

Life had gradually changed for Haucha under the Japanese. The Japanese language and customs had been imposed on the villagers. Their freedoms were restricted, and young men pressed into military service. Although head-hunting was abandoned during the early years of this century, darkness still reigned in their hearts, as they feared the spirits and the night. The shelf for skulls had been removed, but not the feeling of hatred for the outside world.

Money was rare for the Peng family, and often they would be hungry because of crop failure. Typhoons would whip through the mountains, leaving a trail of destruction. Then the whole village would suffer from hunger. But when there was a surplus, or his father found mountain mushrooms or a hive of wild honey, it was Peng's job to carry the produce over the steep trails to the plains.

He had a natural ability to bargain for more cash than anyone else. He was not afraid of the Chinese or Japanese, and always tried for the highest price. He looked forward to these trips to the outside world, for he had a natural curiosity to learn how other people lived. He preferred the river trail that allowed him more time to look around the villages on the plains. He often took the road to Pingtung, miles beyond the village of Santimen to spend a few days. He gained respect from the middlemen who bought from the mountain people, and he learned to face the public fearlessly.

The Second World War brought heartache to the mountain people. Not only were their best young men pressed into military service, but put on the front line of battle. They were the fighting elite and fearless. Their stamina was also superior because of the fitness gained in running up and down the mountain trails with heavy loads. Poverty reigned during these years. To help the

76

war effort, able-bodied farmers were not allowed to cultivate the land, rather they were forced to work in factories on the plains. Fields seen from the air would help enemy bombers to locate inhabited areas so farming was prohibited.

At the close of the war, the Japanese left the island. Few, however, of the young mountain men who had been fighters returned to the mountains. Despair and hunger gripped the people. The fields had been fallow for years, and the villages demoralized by the loss of a generation of young men.

During this time, Peng had grown into a young man, and felt the urgency of the economic situation. But his body was emaciated and malnourished. He could not even work in the fields. As the oldest in the family, he felt the weight of family responsibility.

One day in Haucha, he heard about a new Christian hospital in Pingtung where he could receive free medical help. His family carried him down the mountain trail to Santimen and on to the Pingtung hospital, where he was readily admitted and lovingly attended. Shortly after arrival, the hospital chaplain came to his bedside and gently told him about Jesus Christ. He showed him a picture of a cross and the meaning of salvation. Day after day he came to Peng's bedside and seeing the spiritual hunger in his eyes, pressed the claims of Jesus Christ on his life. Little by little Peng was made aware of his sin and the meaning of repentance and salvation by faith in Jesus Christ. The gospel message penetrated, and Peng accepted Christ as Savior. Day after day as his body healed he was taught the basics of the Christian faith by the chaplain.

The river was full and the current swift as Peng made his way home over the river crossings. When he began the steep climb to Haucha, his feet flew over the trails. He was twenty-two years old, and well at last in body. He exuded the joy he felt in his spirit as he sang on the trail, his voice echoing back to him. Although he heard the bush robins and the distant call of the birds he usually listened for, today these sounds did not register. Now he had new thoughts to consume him. His newfound peace of heart and bubbling joy caused him to laugh aloud. Long before his village was in sight, he had lifted his voice over the valley to shout his arrival. Mother, father, brothers, and sisters ran down the trail to meet him.

He could hardly wait for the family to gather around the low table, set with bowls of millet dumplings and sweet potatoes. Before he began to eat, he asked the whole family to stop while he offered a prayer of thanksgiving to his newfound God. But only Peng bowed his head. The others sat in stony, bewildered silence at the strange behavior of their oldest son.

Peng's mother had had a dream the previous night of the impending return of her son, and the change he would bring to the family and his village. Dreams were an important part of her animistic beliefs and held great weight. To her the dream was a portent of bad things to happen. Although desperately poor and needy herself, she became stonefaced as Peng explained the story of Jesus Christ, and how belief in Him had brought overwhelming peace and joy to his life. He explained that now he knew the God who had created the world, and it was no longer necessary to worship the many objects they worshiped in nature.

"We do not want to change," his mother said to him. "Are not our stone, spirits, and feathers enough for us? You are welcome home, but you must not try to change us to this new religion." The Rukai system is matriarchal and the women make major family decisions. So when Peng had explained all that he had heard in the Pingtung Christian Hospital about Christianity, and had pressed them also to believe, he turned

78

to his mother for the decision of how the family would respond.

"We will be punished if we believe in your God. We will not change, and if you continue to believe, then you must leave our home and village. We do not want to anger the spirits," was her adamant reply. She continued to rail against him, even refusing him food after he returned from the fields and a hard day of labor.

As he slowly walked from his village, hungry and wounded in spirit, his eyes filled with tears. How could he give up what he knew was the only God worthy of his worship? Why couldn't his people and family see the good that Christianity and peace with God would bring to their lives?

And so this remote mountain village of Haucha, in spiritual darkness for hundreds of years, would remain yet longer without a knowledge of the true God. The man whom God had raised up to bring the gospel to his people was sent away, rejected and despised by his own family.

Glenn, Mark, and Keith Winslow pause on the trail to Haucha.

Chapter 10

A Gem in the Rough

Hours later Peng arrived in the city of Kaohsiung. He didn't know anyone, but his footsteps led him to a Christian church. Here he felt sure he would be accepted with love. At the door of the Little Flock Church (an independent Chinese church started by Watchman Nee on mainland China), he was met by a kindly man. When he heard Peng's story of conversion and rejection, he took him in, fed him and gave him a place to stay.

Because Peng had few skills and little education, work was hard to find. However, he was willing, and he had a strong body for manual labor. When Sunday came, he refused to work as he knew his place was in church, where he could worship and learn more about God. Many times on Monday morning he would find himself out of work, because he had refused to work on Sunday. One time he lost his job because he angered the boss, insisting on praying before his meal. Peng was hungry, homesick, and lonely much of the time; but on Sundays he received nurture and love from the Christians at church. In turn he witnessed to whoever would listen. But his heart continually longed for his own people in Haucha, that they might come to know God.

In time, a Christian brother in the church offered him work in a family-owned slipper factory. Here,

among fellow Christians, he was not hindered in growing in his Christian walk, nor discriminated against because of the dark color of his skin or his poor Mandarin
Chinese speech.

One day he heard of meetings to be held in the
Free Methodist church in the nearby town of Fengshan.
The services were especially for mountain people,
geared at giving an intensive one week course on the
basics of the Christian faith. His employer urged him to
attend. There he met other new mountain converts
from the Paiwan tribe. Paul Hsieh was there and a
whole group of other young people. The fellowship
was sweet, and Peng didn't feel embarrassed because
the others knew no more than he about the faith. The
missionaries, Alice and James Taylor, made him feel
welcome.

During one service, with tears in his eyes, Peng
asked for special prayer for the people in his mountain
area, because there were no Christians. He longed for
them to hear.

The Taylors had been aware of the unreached tribal
people in Wutai, and had been praying for the leading
of God to reach this group of people. They knew the
villages were remote, and could only be reached by
hiking eight to ten hours over steep and hazardous
trails. It seemed like a miracle to have this young man
in front of them from that very district, with a burden
for his own people.

The Taylors decided to take an exploration trip into
the neighboring district of Majya. An established church
was working in the Paiwan village across the valley
from Haucha; however, this would be a strategic place
to begin.

In September of 1954, Paul Huang, the Taiwanese
evangelist who spoke Japanese fluently, the James
Taylors, a Paiwan young man named Mr. Lin, and
Peng set off for the first trip into the high mountains.

Peng was happy to be with them and lead the way. It was decided that he should stay in that village and work.

One day the minister from the church in Majya accosted Peng, asking him why he was not more concerned for his own tribal village of Haucha. After all, the only thing he had in common with the Majya people was that he was tribal. Across the valley were his own Rukai people and he could speak their language. He was urged to go fearlessly and witness again to his family.

Peng's heart was overflowing with love for his mountain people as he crossed the valley to his parents' home. "Mother, Father, I've come back!" he exclaimed. He told them again of his growing faith in God, and urged them to consider and believe, also. Their reply was again cold and negative. In spite of his best efforts to persuade them, they refused, and along with the other villagers made fun of him. No one wanted to hear the story of his conversion, let alone of God's love for them.

So Peng went back to the plains and the slipper factory. He could not forget his people, and his heart became more burdened. He argued with God about it and told Him he was too poorly educated and too young to be an effective Christian. But God kept talking with him, and all the while he studied his Bible, growing in spiritual strength. He became confident that when it was God's time, he would be led back to his people.

The missionaries saw Peng's potential, his love for the Lord, and his burden for his own people. They heard his prayers and saw his tears because of the darkness in the Wutai District. They knew he could be released from the slipper factory. So they encouraged him to return again to the Wutai District, not to his own family, where he had twice been rejected, but to continue on over the mountains to the village of Ali. After praying with the missionaries, Peng set out armed with a roll of Sunday school posters depicting the life of Christ, his Bible, and a few provisions.

He passed through Haucha without stopping, taking the trail through the pass, over the swinging bridge and close to the clean mountain pool for which Haucha is named. Although he was tempted to stop and talk with the people there, and slake his thirst before continuing the crisscross path above the village, he barely stopped to glance down at his home as he made his way upward. He had to hurry to reach Ali by dark.

How often he had meandered these paths as a boy, herding his father's goats, many times sitting and dreaming in the hot sunshine. Now he had a mission and goal to share Christ, and as tempted as he was to stop and dream, he couldn't. He passed on by his own family, knowing they would not welcome him nor give him anything to eat. Soon he rounded a turn and could no longer see his village.

The bare mountainside began to change as he entered the deep rain forest, signaling the higher elevation. The air became damp and tropical with thick jungle growth on either side of the trail. Huge trees with manacle-like limbs rose high above, and thick vines cascaded into foliage. It was colder now, and the trail became narrow and slippery. One slip of his foot, and he would fall from the trail a hundred feet down.

As a boy, he had seldom entered this part of the mountain except with a group. It was in these places where the spirits lurked, and no one wanted to startle them. It was imperative that one whisper so as not to set them flying around. But now in defiance, Peng began to sing. The birds, also, kept up a noisy chatter as they prepared for the coming night. Finally, he allowed himself a few minutes' rest before beginning his descent to the village of Ali, a thousand feet below.

Before long he could see the slate roofs gleaming in the late afternoon sun as he hurried toward his goal.

How far God had brought Peng since he first left his village! He had come to Kaohsiung, been accepted and nurtured by fellow Christians, and most importantly had received the call of God to return to his own tribe and preach the gospel. His preparation was minimal by today's standards, but his evangelist's heart was on fire as he arrived to stake the claims of Christ in the village of Ali.

Peng, the seminary student, sets out to witness in the mountains.

Chapter 11

The Polishing

When Peng arrived in Ali, he went directly to the village playground where the water supply was fed by a mountain spring. Here as he drank, he could see both parts of the village nestled, like Haucha, against the mountainside. It appeared about half the size with fifty families. He must hurry, for the mists were coming in from the valley below, and night would soon fall. How could he get the people's attention? He was a stranger in this village. Suddenly, he had the inspiration to sing. He began in a clear, resonant voice, "Joy to the world, the Lord is come, let earth receive her king."

People, returning from the fields at dusk, were struck still on the trails and mesmerized by his voice and words. Instead of going to their homes, they turned to the school yard where already a crowd of children was surrounding Peng. As the people came, he stopped singing and began to preach. He felt God's strength surging through him, giving him the words to say.

"Jesus Christ has come into the world. Believe in Him and receive the joy He wants to give you. I have come to tell you about Jesus Christ. Man is a sinner. You cannot see God with your eyes. You cannot see sin. Nevertheless, you are sinners and have committed many sins — thieves, liars, murderers, you deserve hell. But God loves you. God is the creator of the universe and the nature that we have been worshiping as god. We must worship the true God, rather than what He has made. If you believe in Him and in His Son Jesus Christ, you will be saved from your sins."

For a short time the people listened intently, and then their interest turned to anger. Two young men, who were cousins named Lo and Ou, became violent in their dislike and hurled insult after insult at Peng. Parents drew their children aside to take them home. The spirits would be coming with the mists to cause harm.

Peng was soon left standing alone in the school yard. He had nowhere to go. This did not bother him, as he felt the presence of the Lord. The words he had spoken had not come from him, but directly from God. Then out of the darkness stepped Mr. Bau, offering him shelter and food for the night. All evening Peng exhorted the Bau family.

Peng was up at sunrise ready to leave. He still had two villages to visit. Chunu was down the trail, half an hour's hike on the Japanese-constructed road. It was smaller than Ali with only twenty-five families. He went resolutely to the school yard, again drawing a crowd by singing and then preaching. He did not feel a warm welcome, but no one rejected him. Again a man came forward to offer the stranger a place and food for the night. Peng used these hours to witness.

The next day leaving the wide Japanese trail, Peng made a sharp descent into the valley below, where Tawu village nestles against the steep mountain along a river. The trail was precipitous and dangerous, with sharp sudden drops to the valley. He headed for the school yard and proclaimed the same message: "If we believe in Jesus, we can have forgiveness for our sins."

Tawu was a proud village with a long history. Again the response was anger and fear. Next to the school yard was a police post manned by policemen assigned

88

by the government to keep law and order. Because of the anger of the people, Peng was taken to the police station, where he was charged with gathering a crowd and preaching without permission.

"I have the right to preach because I am a Christian. Jesus was persecuted just as you are persecuting me. He was even killed by his enemies," was his defense. Finally, he was released and another kind family took him to their home for the night.

That night Peng reflected on the three villages where he had left the gospel message. Should he return to Kaohsiung and report to the Taylors, or should he go back again to Ali and Chunu to continue to preach the gospel? He knew that he had received God's greatest gift, salvation from sin. He had faith that his fellow tribesmen would also accept the Way, the Truth, and the Life. He resolved to continue preaching, and knew that God would honor His Word.

Three times Peng returned to the three villages. Each time he was made welcome in the three homes that had welcomed him before. But outside these homes he was railed, insulted, and mocked. He was told repeatedly by the police not to return, but there was nothing they could do, as he was a tribal man and had free access to all the mountain villages. God's Word sustained him, and he resolved to follow His leading at any cost. He asked himself, though, how he was to continue to preach without believers, a home, or money? He decided to return to Kaohsiung, where he knew he could work in the slipper factory and make money for another evangelistic trip to the Wutai District.

In Kaohsiung, the Taylors were excited by the account of Peng's fearless witness to his people. They could see that here was a man of God's calling, and through him was an unprecedented opportunity for evangelism. In the midst of spirit worship and mysticism, the seed of the gospel had been planted. Now was the time to pluck the fruit and establish a Free Methodist church in the Wutai District.

God had been blessing the work on the plains as well. In the interval from 1952 to 1957, the work had expanded from two preaching points to twenty churches and chapels and twelve preaching points. In 1953 the total membership was 128, rising by 1957 to 662, and then doubling again by 1959.

Holy Light Theological College had been established in the fall of 1955 to train workers and preachers to serve the rapidly growing churches. Among the school's first group of students were the mountain young people from the Paiwan tribal area, who had been converted in Tsaopu. These young men studied during the week and returned on weekends to their districts to preach.

Peng was enrolled in the first class. He traveled to the villages in the Wutai area over weekends. Monday mornings he would begin the long trip back to school — eight hours of walking and two hours by bus to Kaohsiung. He would spend Tuesday through Friday mornings in class, and Friday afternoon he would begin the long trip again walking fifty miles to cover the villages in three days.

With the encouragement of monthly financial support from the missionaries, he returned to Ali, passing through his home village of Haucha. He had memorized the verse in God's Word about honoring his father and mother. Now he wanted to return to tell them of his plans to work full time for the Lord. As he approached the mountain pass and doorway to his village, he felt led to give his parents his first month's wages.

He waited with bated breath to see their reaction. They received it gratefully, but still were not willing to embrace the Christian faith.

90

"You may believe in Jesus if you wish, even though we cannot," they said. Peng was much encouraged by these words, for they showed that although his parents were not yet ready, at least they did not oppose him as bitterly as they had before.

The next day Peng headed up the mountain trail to Ali. He was welcomed in the Bau home, and offered a place to stay on his weekend trips. The Bau family was royalty according to the tribal system. Mr. Bau was the traditional headman, and his wife a princess. Their living room was the largest in Ali. On the walls were the jawbones of the many boar he had killed, as well as his weapons, spears, and guns. Along one wall were hundreds of clay pots used for food storage. A large area of slate-covered floor was adequate for seating thirty people. The courtyard was also spacious enough for any overflow.

After the Bau family accepted Christ, they invited their neighbors to do the same. In the first four months of Peng's intensive preaching in Ali, there were more than thirty converts.

God blessed his efforts in Chunu and Tawu as well, giving him forty believers in Chunu and fifty in Tawu in the first few months of his ministry. The harvest was ripe for reaping.

Peng, the evangelist, always has a smile!

Chapter 12

Gems from the Gem

For two years Peng kept up his rigorous schedule of schooling and evangelism. He was dependent on the Lord for his food and clothing, for needed strength to travel by foot over long miles and difficult, treacherous trails. He loved the people and felt compassion for them because of their physical ailments. He would often carry the sick on his back for eight hours to the plains for medical help. Because Christ's love was radiating through Peng, his people were attracted to Christianity.

Two of the young men who had opposed the gospel in Ali were the cousins, Lo and Ou. Lo was twenty-seven when Peng first came. By mountain standards, he had had an excellent education. He had attended the Japanese school in his village, and had excelled in speech and reading. As a lad he had been carried on his Japanese teacher's back to a speech contest on the plains, where he took first place. He had attended an agricultural school, and then returned to his father's farm in Ali. Like Peng, he had worked on the construction of the Japanese road, which reached over the mountain from Haucha and down to Wutai, the capital of the district.

At first, Lo was adamantly opposed to his young bride attending Peng's meetings in the headman's home. At this time, many relief goods were being distributed in the mountains by various organizations. One was a Catholic organization, and it was said that only if people were willing to become Catholic, and register as such, could they receive free food and clothing. With Lo's advanced education, he was suspicious of this group and also questioned Peng's ulterior motives. He never missed an opportunity to deride Peng and engage him in debate. Peng always stayed calm, and seemed to have the answer to each argument. Lo, and his cousin Ou, would scheme throughout the week to trip him up, but each weekend Peng came, he always had a ready answer.

After Lo's wife became a believer, Lo grudgingly began to attend the services with her. When she became pregnant, the age-old superstition gripped their hearts that something would be wrong with the child. Out of fear that his wife's new God would do something to the baby, Lo believed nominally. He still loved to drink and smoke, and spent hours carousing with Ou and their friends.

Lo continued to attend the services, and was much relieved when his wife delivered a normal boy. One night while he was in the Bau home waiting for the service to begin, someone thrust a Bible into his hands and asked him to preach. His reputation for public speaking had followed him. He gripped the Bible and looked at the verses. It all became a blur. He saw himself as filthy rags with all his sins wheeling in front of him. His tongue stuck to the roof of his mouth, and for the first time in twenty-seven years, he was speechless.

That night he had a dream. In the dream he saw a tall man wearing white robes. This man told him that of all the people going to the Bau home, he was the most evil. Awakening, he knew it was Peng's Jesus Christ speaking to him. He shared his dream with his cousin Ou and discussed the implications with him. They could hardly wait for Peng to arrive that weekend. How

94

jubilant Peng was to interpret the dream, and prayer-fully he led these two young men in the sinner's prayer. They wept with joy and embraced Peng as they felt freedom from sin. Neither man drank nor smoked after that. Their conversion made an impression on the entire village, and soon Bau's home was too small for meetings. A church building was planned.

Tang, another of the village's early converts, was younger than Lo and Ou when he heard about Jesus Christ. He had had a difficult childhood. His mother had been caught in the roar of a landslide, and along with three others was swept to her death. Three years later, his father was cutting wood on the mountainside. The knife had slipped, cutting a vital artery in his leg. Slowly, with a tourniquet applied, he crawled home. But it was too late, and two weeks later he, too, had died.

Tang, the oldest of five, was left to scratch out a living in the hillside fields. He set to work to keep the family together, even though the relatives wanted to separate them. Tang was clever in school and should have had the chance to continue on the plains, but he was too poor.

He heard about the Catholics bringing food and clothing to Ali, and quickly registered his brothers and sisters in the Catholic faith. He also joined, but sat in Mass, understanding nothing that was said. He was miserable and unhappy with his lot.

One night at dark his little sister came running, telling him about someone from the village of Haucha who was relating a story about a man who gives everything anyone needs. Tang hurried to the school yard and was amazed at the story of love.

Tang attended the services in the headman's home, and became one of the first in Ali to believe. His mind opened to the gospel and light penetrated his intellect and heart.

Peng saw the potential in these three young men —
Tang, Lo, and Ou, and encouraged them to consider
studying at Holy Light. For Tang, the decision was easy
because it would give him the opportunity to pursue
the dream of an education. As for Lo and Ou, they felt
the need of further instruction in the Word. Peng joyfully took them to Kaohsiung to introduce them to the
missionaries.

All three were readily accepted into Holy Light. Lo
was especially bright, and finished the four-year program in two years. During his time at Holy Light, Lo
lightened Peng's load by pastoring in Tawu on
weekends. Ou pastored in Chunu, and Tang took over
the leadership of the flock in Ali. God blessed these
three men's ministries, and they became spiritual leaders of their people.

Peng was now free to seek new villages where
there was no gospel witness. But first he returned to
Haucha to visit his family and rest. He also wanted to
find a wife from his home. By this time the Presbyterian church had begun intensive evangelism in the
Wutai District, and had entered the villages of Wutai,
Jyamu, and Ilase. They had also gone to Haucha and
found a spiritually hungry group of people. However,
Peng's own family were still not believers.

When Peng returned home, he found that his
mother was ill and needed medical care. Not only was
she sick physically, but she was often seized with trem-
ors, causing unconsciousness. During the seizures, she
could be heard conversing with the spirits which con-
vulsed her body. Others could also hear these voices.
The devils told her that Peng was coming to get them.
Peng knew the forces of evil were strong in his mother,
yet he had the faith to believe that God wanted to release her from these forces. He put his hands on her
and prayed. She quieted down and fell into a natural
sleep. His father, watching, exclaimed, "Our son's God

is strong!'' Peng rejoiced because he knew that his father's heart was softening.

Peng lovingly carried his mother on his back down the steep trail from Haucha to the Pingtung Christian Hospital, where he himself had received medical care. Before leaving her, he sensed she was ready to believe. How sweet was her conversion. Peng hurried back to Haucha to tell his father, who soon said, "I, too, need your God." One by one all his brothers were converted until the entire family believed.

In his home village of Haucha, Peng met a lovely young girl who had become a committed Christian. The night of his wedding feast was one long to be remembered. According to past tradition, drinking and carousing were always important parts of the celebration. When he told the guests that there was to be none of that at his feast, they were amazed that he could be happy without that kind of festivity. Peng and his bride were able to demonstrate the difference belief in Christ made and show that some of their cultural traditions had negative effects on their lives.

When his wife became pregnant with their first child, the unbelievers told him that because of his belief in the new God, his child would be born with three arms or some other deformity. Eventually, Peng and his wife had five normal, healthy children, dispelling the fears of malformed children being born to Christians.

In time Peng's younger sister became engaged to a man from Maer, the Paiwan village which for many years had been the bitter enemy of Haucha. She was to marry a man whose father had unsuccessfully laid in ambush to kill Peng's father thirty-seven years before. Over the years hatred for this Paiwan man in Maer had seethed in Peng's heart. But now with Christ in his life, the hatred was gone.

Peng was asked to perform the wedding ceremony. When the elders from the two villages met for the formal marriage decision, Peng stood up and said, "As you know our tribes have been enemies. Thirty-seven years ago, some of your men tried to kill my father. The Bible teaches that we are to forgive our enemies. So now, I freely forgive you. As a symbol of my forgiveness, I give my sister in marriage to a young man in your tribe whose father tried to kill my father years ago. This is the change Christianity has made in our lives."

Real changes did indeed take place in the lives of the Rukai people. Their newly found love for the Lord Jesus replaced their fear of the spirits. Miracle by miracle they were convinced that the God they now worshiped was superior to their nature deities.

As they listened to the gospel, they realized they did not need to hate and fear, but could live at peace with all men. Their lifestyles changed as the claims of Christ were accepted. Their bodies became the temples of a holy God. No longer did they drink, smoke, or chew betel nut. From the money saved they could buy food, clothes, and medicine for their families. Their lives became wonderfully different through this dimension of belief in Jesus Christ. They were new men and women.

Peng and his believing parents.

Chapter 13

Peng, the Evangelist

"Look at this Japanese shrine," said Peng to James Taylor III. They paused to rest along the trail on their way to Tawu. Behind the cement slab shrine, in a partially covered grave, lay the bony remains of a Japanese expedition that had traveled into the mountains to examine the vast supply of camphor laurel. The headhunters had won the encounter.

Late in the day as the sun sank behind the towering peaks, Peng and Taylor arrived in Tawu where they would conduct the first of several services to be held that weekend in the Wutai District.

The oil lamps flickered from the ceiling as Christians gathered to hear Taylor's message. He spoke in Mandarin, and Peng interpreted into Rukai. Before long the little mountain room was full, and many were standing outside. The service was simple with songs and choruses. Posters depicting Jesus' life were shown, and their message translated into the Rukai dialect. How different was the attitude of the tribesmen now, compared to fifty years ago when many Japanese had lost their heads. Now hearts were open to the love of Christ, and the task of the church was about to expand — building and nurturing the Rukai people in the faith.

Helping and encouraging this young church was James Hudson Taylor III, who, with his wife, Leone, arrived in Taiwan in 1955. Young and energetic, with a mastery of the Chinese language, he was the natural one in the China Free Methodist Mission to assist in the evangelistic efforts of the Taiwan Annual Conference established in 1955. James Taylor III not only taught in the Bible school during the week, but often accompanied Peng on the fifty-mile trek on weekends to Ali, Chunu, and Tawu.

The churches in Wutai were waiting to be built. The Sunday schools and youth needed programs; laymen needed training; a hymnbook and the Scriptures needed translation; these and many more tasks awaited accomplishment.

In time, William Bicksler, John Silva, and Harry Winslow all helped to build a strong mountain church.

Pastor Peng, now ordained and with adequate help, was excited about a government project to move more than fifty families down to a dry riverbed on the plains, where they would reclaim the rocky land, and make it arable farmland. Several families from the Rukai village had been asked to volunteer. The government was becoming increasingly interested in helping with the economic plight of the people, and this was a good pilot project.

The plans called for installing electricity, building a road into the heart of the mountains to facilitate communications, and mining marble. The government wanted to promote tourism and access to the outside world for the mountain people. The needs of each village were assessed, and in some cases the only course for helping a village was to move the entire village out of the mountains to the plains, or to another area of the mountains.

During the Japanese era, the river had been harnessed behind a huge dyke, where the two major rivers converged. Behind this dyke were miles of dry, rocky untillable land. Knowing the industrious, hardworking nature of the mountain tribes, the government offered this land to them to reclaim.

One of the early Christians, who had provided a home for Pastor Peng in Chunu, suggested that he help with this project during its crucial beginning stages. A pioneering and cheerful spirit was needed, along with backbreaking effort to remove the rocks. The new village was appropriately named "Rock Village."

The land was divided into plots, and lots were drawn by the people for the plot selection. Pastor Peng drew one for himself, as well as the church. Then the tremendous job of removing the rocks began. He endeared himself even more to his fellow tribesmen as he worked beside them, slowly bringing life back to the riverbed. Some people felt it an impossible task, and abandoned their land. The lots were again divided and given to those who remained.

Before starting the church, Pastor Peng invited missionary Geneva Sayre to come from Kaohsiung and conduct children's meetings. They became the highlight of the week for the village. Not only children, but adults came to hear the stories. It was not long before Pastor Peng's evangelistic zeal bore fruit. Soon after the houses of the people were built, the first church was constructed in 1964.

All the land yielded the first year was a poor crop of potatoes and more rocks. Malnutrition glazed the skin of the children. There was little water, and what did come from the nearby river was dirty and undrinkable.

Taiwan Christian Service, a service organization to assist people in many ways, came to the rescue. They sent a team to search the riverbed for a well deep enough to sustain this large area. What a joyous day it was for John Silva, Pastor Peng, and the people when that water was found. It was enough, not only for irrigation purposes, but for their houses. Taiwan Christian Service also helped plan the irrigation system, as well as begin a pilot project to raise piglets.

John Silva's wife, Ellen, came and brought medicine, food, and clothing to help them through the difficult days in beginning a new village.

In time, the village was divided into three parts, based on tribal dialects. From Rock Village it was officially renamed "Three Harmony Village." The land slowly began to produce, as the rocks were removed and new topsoil brought in. Fruit trees were planted, and gradually the "village of rocks" was transformed into beautiful green fields, yielding two crops a year.

The church soon became too small. It had become the center for the Rukai mountain people. The church held monthly workers' meetings, large rallies for the youth, and retreats. Plans developed to make it into the center for the Rukai District of the Free Methodist Annual Conference. In 1982, a beautiful two-story church was built. With the exception of a gift from the Japan Free Methodist Conference, the money for the new building came from the Rukai people, and the work was donated by the members.

After the new church was completed, Pastor Peng was relocated to evangelize in another river valley in which there were three villages. Each village spoke a different language. Undaunted, using Japanese, Pastor Peng went with his young wife and three small children to Wanshan. Because his wife's health was broken with tuberculosis, she nearly died several times, so Pastor Peng took her to the Pingtung Christian Hospital, where she received good food, rest, and care. Unswerving in his love for Christ, he returned alone to minister God's love to the people.

Several families from the villages of Ali, Chunu, and Tawu had moved away from their high mountain homes, seeking better land in the lowlands on the east coast near Taitung. Others settled with them. Pastor Peng was again asked to relocate to begin a church work among the people in Tanan. His evangelistic zeal, and ability to suffer hardship, was a well-known fact. Leaving Wanshan in the capable hands of one of his converts, Pastor Lu, Pastor Peng with his family made another major move. Soon there was a strong nucleus of believers in Tanan.

Pastor Peng has introduced hundreds in his tribe to Christ. He established seven churches in ten years of evangelistic fervor. Driven by his family from his home, he relentlessly returned again and again to his Rukai people to share God's love. He suffered hardship and never complained. Always, his smile said, "I love you, and so does God."

Today he is pastoring in his home village of Haucha, where there's a beautiful new church built on the cliff above the river.

In this part of the story of the mountains which sing of God's love, I have told of the nationals who brought Christ to their people. Read on to learn more, especially of Peng's social involvement with his people, and how he helped this writer to see people's needs, and to see how the church could enter a ministry of physical as well as spiritual healing.

Near the Miracle Church, James H. Taylor III and Chinese evangelist Timothy Tsao baptize converts.

Missionary Geneva Sayre's children's meetings became the highlight of the week.

Pastor Peng (second row, left) and relatives in front of the new Haucha church.

104

Part III

Love Wears Hiking Boots

Ruth Winslow (center) hiking to Haucha with Harry, Glenn, Sheri Williams (Dr. Dave Williams's daughter), and helpers.

Ruth Winslow leads a mothers' class; Pastor Peng interprets into the Rukai dialect.

Chapter 14

To Care Enough

The first time I went to the village of Tawu with my husband, Harry, I was approached by a mountain mother who tried to give me one of her babies. The baby, the smaller of twins, was clutched in her arms. The child weighed under five pounds and showed signs of malnutrition, with the old wrinkled look and leathery skin. Perhaps it was dehydration which made her look so tiny, frail, and helpless, obviously sick, and certainly getting the short end of her mother's scant milk supply.

I remember the mother dejectedly explaining to me that she already had her hands full with several other children, and not enough food for them. It was more than she could do to produce the milk needed for these additional babies. Pastor Lo confirmed that hers was one of the needier families in the village.

She wanted me to take one — the small one. I could have her for keeps, could give her away, or bring her back when she was healthy and bigger. This was my first trip into the mountains, and I didn't even have a stethoscope along. I looked at Harry, but I already knew in my heart that our answer to her would have to be "No."

Unfortunately, we were too new to mountain work to know of the marvelous organization Lillian Dickson had founded called Mustard Seed which took care of this kind of baby.

"No," I told her, "I'll not be able to take your baby, but I promise I'll send back milk powder, baby food, and vitamins. Be sure to attend the health classes I'll be having so you can learn why your baby is this way, and how to prevent health problems with your children."

Having answered her, we began the eight-hour hike back to the plains and our home in Pingtung. I did send her milk powder and liquid vitamins with the returning mountain guide.

A month later we were in Tawu, and I looked for the mother with the twins. She was there all right, but with only one baby in her arms.

I had cared, but not enough. She needed so much more than milk and vitamins. I felt I had failed. The mothers didn't blame me because they were resigned to the fact that up to half of their babies might die. But I blamed myself for I felt I had handled the situation badly. It might have had a different ending. I was accountable to these mothers, as well as to God. I had to make plans carefully to help them with their needs.

Not long after that we were in the village of Haucha, where Harry was having evangelistic meetings. We arrived in the village just in time to participate in the funeral of a newborn daughter of one of the elders who had just carried our things up the precipitous mountain. She had died with hyaline membrane disease. This was the couple's third baby to die with the same symptoms. The father hadn't even been able to share the pain and sorrow with his wife, who had delivered a seemingly normal child, only to have it die so soon afterward. At least we could participate in the graveside service.

Later I went to Mrs. Chen's home to sit, along with the other mountain women, and share her grief. Embracing her, I rocked back and forth trying to mete her some measure of comfort. I promised her a hospital delivery the next time so that her baby could get care. Later when she was pregnant again, I made sure she was taken to the Pingtung Christian Hospital where she did deliver a healthy baby.

When she returned with her baby to her mountain home, she said, "Thank you, Teacher-Mother. You are the first one to care enough to help." For years her words echoed in my mind every time I felt my tired muscles, bleeding blisters, and the weariness of the long mountain hikes.

After studying Mandarin Chinese, Harry was assigned by the Taiwan Annual Conference as an adviser to the young mountain churches of the Rukai and Paiwan tribes. We lived in Pingtung, a town ten miles from the base of the mountains. On clear days, especially during the rainy season, we could see the green mountains whose peaks pierced the clouds.

When Harry returned from his first trip, he spoke with enthusiasm for the work, and the spiritual ministry which he could contribute. However, he also felt frustration as he stepped out of the pulpit and was surrounded by the physical needs of the people. Mothers, with babies in their arms, children on their backs, and perhaps others clutching their skirts, would come and ask for remedies for the hurts of their children. They would repeatedly ask the same question, "Can you help?"

I listened carefully, and felt the deep down stirring of memories begin to surface — memories of similar needs seen when I was a young teenager in India. Longings were aroused that had more recently been suppressed because of family and motherhood duties.

I had seen pain and suffering as a young girl in both China and India. That was the reason I was now a missionary nurse. In China, when I was nine, I had been greatly moved by a blind beggar boy my age who had asked for something to eat. He came to our door at noontime. I had responded by sitting beside him on our front steps, heaping his bowl with noodles. I had also eaten my noodles, pondering the dilemma of a boy my age with no family, no home, hungry, and totally blind. Something inside my little girl's heart reached out to him, and we felt love for one another. My mother had said I could prepare to be a missionary right then. So I operated on my doll Mary, and carried aspirin and water to any ailing family members, pretending to know a great deal about medicine.

I had helped missionary nurse Myra Martin in the villages in India; and she, knowing the Lord was preparing my young heart, allowed me to change the leprous dressings, and treated me as her equal. I understood heartache, and would weep with her over the sight of a newborn baby dying from tetanus, wrapped in dirty rags and lying on a floor spread with cowdung.

As a girl of sixteen, I found fulfillment in Jesus Christ. Alone in the night, in the dells of Hebron School in the Nilgiris Mountains of South India, I made a complete surrender of myself to the lordship of Christ in my life. When I resumed my visits to the villages with Myra Martin on my next holiday, I was amazed at the change in myself. Not only did I see the hurting bodies, but the empty look in the eyes of the people — a look that their Hindu gods could not fill. I had become aware of spiritual hurts as well.

At last, after years of schooling, with a sensitive, loving husband, language preparation, and three small children, I was able to begin to fulfill my dream of helping people, at least on a part-time basis.

What of the children? Glenn, Mark, and Keith were ages five, four, and two. I could certainly stand a break from them from time to time. Their healthy little bodies and minds were inexhaustible wellsprings of energy, moving through my days at maximum velocity. They seemed to keep one step ahead of their mother in mischief. Normally it would be impossible for a young mother like me to leave her children for three days once a month. But other missionary mothers are not fortunate enough to have both sets of parents on the mission field with them at the same time. Harry's mother, Carolyn Winslow, lived just a street away in Pingtung; and my parents, William and Evangeline Smith, were teaching at Holy Light, fifteen miles north in Kaohsiung. They were happy to have some action, especially when it would end in a few days. Besides, I soon discovered that loving Grandmother Winslow had a calming effect on the boys. At least for a few days after living with her, they were angelic, pious, and the epitome of good behavior.

Later when their little legs developed, we found they could keep one step ahead of us on the trail, often running ahead and back to see why we were so slow. We found the fresh air, mountain streams, and water holes inexhaustible entertainment for them. They would carry the doctor's bag, observe the clinic outdoors from a tree overhead, or help count pills. Our boys came to love the mountain people, and received mutual love in return.

That problem was solved. But what of the distance involved, the climbing and the long fifty-mile trek? Could I do it? None of our Free Methodist missionary women had yet climbed to the tribes in the Wutai District.

It wasn't hard to respond. My life, since a girl in India's mountains where I had gone to school, had been in preparation for this moment. I was strong and healthy, with a good constitution. From my angle there in Pingtung, those mountains didn't seem so high. Anyway, the song that kept ringing through my mind as I prepared to go with Harry on his next trip was from The Sound of Music:

"Climb every mountain, ford every stream, follow every rainbow . . . "

111

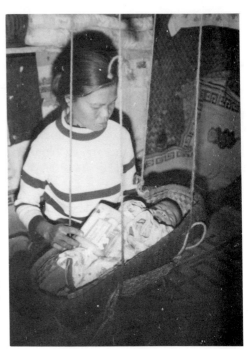

Rukai mother and baby in
hanging basket bed.

Ruth Winslow at a clinic with her stethoscope.

Chapter 15

Love Wears Hiking Boots

"Cross every bridge" should have been added to the song, because bridges became very much a part of my life in the years that followed.

For the first year and a half we had no car. Since the only road into this section of the mountains was not in the direction of our villages, that fact didn't bother us much. The government had long-range plans for roads and bridges into the heart of the Wutai District, where it planned to promote tourism and mine marble. The first section was completed in 1967. That was a two-hundred-yard cement bridge, crossing a huge river at the town of Santimen.

Half a mile east of this river, two smaller rivers converged. Our mountain villages were deep in the recesses of the mountains, which rose steeply out of these river valleys. Wutai, Ali, Tawu, and Chunu were along the one river at different elevations, and Haucha was high over the other river. In the sixteen years (including furloughs) I worked in these mountains, I saw the road built to the farthest village of Ali and the village of Haucha moved down to the river, where a suspension bridge had been built on a beautiful plateau along the river. A vehicular road and bridge were also built to the new Haucha. From 1967 to 1982, we watched and participated in the progress of the government in opening up the mountains.

113

After we had a car, we would drive a little farther each trip, and thus cut down on our walking time. The new road was dirt and gravel with a big rut down the middle, and wide enough in most places for just one car. At first there were no guardrails or embankments. The road snaked its way around the mountains, along cliff edges with thousand-foot drops. The grades were steep, and we never knew if we would be able to bring our car safely down the mountain, especially during the rainy season. We always carried picks and shovels for the landslides and falling rocks, which were common impediments to our arriving at the end of the new road.

When it was time to hike, long inactive climbing muscles and lungs and feet were what gave me the most trouble at first. The trails seemed to go on forever, although it was a mere twenty-six miles to Haucha on the upper trail, and another twenty-five down from Tawu, with several miles between the villages. We hiked straight up or straight down, as well as along stretches at high elevation on the level trails. What we gained in an hour of steep staircase climbing would be lost the next by the rapid, slithery descent to the river.

As I did not have proper hiking boots, I wore my worn nursing shoes which had comfortably tramped many hospital corridors in the United States, but certainly had never climbed mountains. They were smooth soled, as were the slate rocks, and often found themselves in conflict. I would be the loser and find myself down on my posterior, with my long legs dangling out over the mountainside.

Being a prim and proper missionary, I attempted at first to hike in skirts. Mountain women wear skirts which cover their knees, but under them are sensible leggings tied below the knee. I never saw a mountain man or woman fall, but on one wet trip, during which we descended from the mountain pass above Haucha to Ali, I fell nine times because of my shoes — the last time lacerating my hand as I reached out for a clump of grass and grabbed razor sharp slate. And those shoes caused me a lot more grief before I joyfully committed them to the river just before my first furlough. With continual wettings they shrank; and my feet in their prison cells were cramped, with blisters open and bleeding, toenails black and bruised, and corns and callouses pressing like nails into the raw flesh. In time, my skirts were replaced by culottes in the summer and slacks in the winter.

Now I must take my readers on a typical trip and let you share the excitement and joy, as well as the pain, of love wearing hiking boots.

After climbing for several hours, we make a rapid descent to the river, where we come to our first swinging bridge. Because it is typical of hundreds of bridges in the mountains, it bears describing. It is a hundred feet long, spanning a narrow gorge a hundred feet deep. The river below is fed by countless mountain streams, and roars in a rapid descent to the sea. Its moods change with the seasons. In dry winter months, it becomes aqua colored, and the white side and rocks can be clearly seen as it moves lazily along. In the rainy season it is dark and ferocious in its dash to the sea.

Ordinary clothesline wire wound together form one to two-inch cables which hold up the bridge. Both ends are buried in cement and rock on either side of the mountain. Wire is laced and suspended from the cables forming a cradle through which boards are placed. Many of the boards are rotten and some are missing. Sometimes there are three boards abreast, sometimes two, but often only one. It appears they are well woven and secured, but it is best not to count on it. If you don't step in the middle of the board, one end may come up to meet you. Your stomach twists as you see the river below. It seemed I was the only one disturbed by those loose boards. Pastor Peng helped me across the first time, telling me to keep my eyes on the distant end and not to look down. How I could do that and check out the safety of the boards, I never knew; but later I learned to be first in line and not get caught in the convulsions of the bridge as many people crossed together.

During our early mountain trips that bridge broke when the cable snapped, sending fifteen mountain people plunging to the river below. The carefully balanced bundles on tops of heads and backs fell. The carriers clutched and slipped, slipped and clutched at shreds of wire and broken rotting planks. Only the young and quick could hold on, desperately pulling themselves up and inching their way to the other side, their hearts torn for their friends struggling in the current below. Only one of the seven who fell into the river survived. This one, who was a Christian, testified that as he fell, he cried, "God save me!" Just then a hand appeared, and he did not feel his impact with the water. When he became conscious, he was on the shore.

Soon after this we again returned to the mountains. When we came to the broken bridge, we had to slide carefully down the steep cliff side to the water's edge, where a bamboo raft awaited travelers. Nine strands of wound clothesline wire formed a cable pulley stretching across the river. To keep the raft from being carried down the stream, our carriers attached a rope to the wire and we were pulled across.

There was another way to cross the river before the new bridge was built. We had our chance to cross this way one evening at dusk, at the height of a savage typhoon. We had to climb into an oversized bird cage, suspended from a cable pulley which spanned the river. Because the torrential typhoon rains had caused the river to rise rapidly and swiftly, the raft was out of the question.

We had been in Haucha for three days. The mountain people, knowing the seasons and the signs of an impending typhoon, had warned us to stay on a day and let the big wind pass. But we had wanted to return to our children in Pingtung and lacked the experience and knowledge of the mountaineers.

At our insistence we set out with Pastor Peng's old father as our guide. After a couple of hours on the trail, we realized that what they had warned us of was truly a powerful wind, with accompanying rains. High on the side of the mountain, we clung together as we faced the wind, taking shelter for a few moments in the lee of the mountain, only to face the wind again at the next corner. I remember the snakes and lizards scurrying across our path, seeking shelter in the rocks.

The streams which a few days before had been sweet little rivulets that allowed us to slake our thirst and wet our towels, were now uncrossable raging torrents, falling from the cliff above. To attempt to cross would be to be swept over the side of the mountain.

We were completely dependent on our guide to find an alternate route. He climbed up the side of the mountain to find a safer place to cross. I can still feel the grip of his hand on mine as he said, "Put your foot exactly where I put mine and you will be safe." He knew a strong rock from a loose one. This was the man who had so adamantly opposed his son's turning to Christianity, and who could tell many a tale of earlier head-hunting escapades. I never let my eyes stray a moment as I watched his feet and followed his footsteps. I trusted my mountain guide completely. I dared not think of the river ahead.

When we arrived at the river we saw our means of conveyance — the "bird cage!" After battling the storm all afternoon, we considered it just one more obstacle

117

in the race to get home. Knowing that the weight of the cable was built for the mountain man, and because I was lighter, Harry made me go first. We clutched hands, kissed, and said a prayer. I was locked in my cage and went down, down, down. The river rushed up to meet me. As I slowly swung to a stop, I realized my body weight had carried me half way down and I was now dangling like a little doll over the middle of the river. I felt the black empty sensation of nothingness as the wind whipped through the gorge, buffeting my little cage. The rain lashed down so hard I could see neither shore. I had the feeling that the river was swirling not too far beneath my feet, and I straightened my legs and clutched my walking stick to me.

Suddenly, I had a clear sensation of the words of the Psalm of David sweep over me, "Underneath are the everlasting arms"; and calm came to the frightened bird in its cage. Very soon I was moving again as I felt my cage being pulled steadily toward the other side. Getting out, I sank to the nearest rock to watch and pray as Harry went through the same ordeal. Again we clung to each other in relief and thankfulness to God.

Late that night after we had buffeted several more hours of hiking in the rain, wind, and dark, we made it back to Pingtung. Our parents were shocked to see us.

"Our foolish children," they said, "do you not know that the eye has passed our town?" The next day in the peace that follows a typhoon, we discovered that the eye likely had passed through that mountain valley the same afternoon we were hiking home.

All of our trips, fortunately, were not filled with that kind of dangerous excitement. Most of the time the weather was beautiful and the mountain air invigorating. Climbing to the pinnacles where we could see the distant ranges or the curling rivers below not only hardened our bodies and conditioned us physically, but gave us the insatiable desire to keep climbing, to come

118

back and expose ourselves again and again to the grandeur of God's handiwork.

Thinking about coming into Haucha village at dusk makes me recall a sensation which brings the tears to my eyes as I write. I think of the many times we arrived after a full day of climbing. We were often joined on the trail during the last part of our journey by children who had come to meet us. We heard the calls of welcome echoing over the valley from people we heard but could not see. They knew we were coming to help them. The welcome was an ancient tune and soon over, but the echo continued until it reached us. Suddenly the trail sliced through two rock formations, and we were at the icy mountain pool for which Haucha is named.

Children ran up to meet and stare at us. Crossing the old rickety bridge, their cries would be welcomed, lightening our bodies as we walked onto the school yard. Below us were the terraced rows of a hundred slate homes. We could still smell the fresh air, but now it was tinged with the smell and fragrance of the villagers preparing their main meal for the day.

Gratefully, we appeared at the pastor's door, where there was a warm welcome. Hot water laced with honey, the inviting warmth of the kitchen fire and slate beds, hard as they may become at 3:00 a.m., at that moment of arrival beckoned to our bodies to stretch a moment and rest.

We loved living with the people. They had so little of this world's goods yet shared what they had. One large, long room hugged the mountain wall. Opposite this wall was a row of windows looking out over distant mountains. Built against the back wall was a ledge for sleeping, elevated one foot off the slate-covered floor. There the whole family slept, except the grandparents whose place was on the floor by the fire. A curtain could be pulled across the sleeping area to shelter it from the peering eyes of children, always insatiably curious about the foreigners. On top of the slate bed our hostess laid padded quilts. Often there were ten of us in the room at night. If it rained and stormed, the dogs and goats would join the family.

Sleeping with such a large group always produced a cacophony of sound worthy of study. The human noises were the dyspneic breathing and wheezing of the old folks and the sighing, snoring, and coughing of all ages. The unhuman noises were created by the scratchings of dogs and fowl and the running patter of rats over the slate rooftops. Sometimes the rats came inside and scurried over our feet and around our heads. We usually hung our backpacks high on a nail to outwit them, especially if there were food for the trail. I often lay on my slate bed wishing for a pen and paper to compose a symphony to a rat. Mostly, though, we were too tired to let those little things bother us. Sleep claimed our bodies early, for it was at dawn our work would begin.

Finishing our spiritual or healing ministry in that village, on we went to the next village. As we climbed the steep trail, at superficial observation we could not see where to put our next footstep. However, every mountain man knew the exact toehold at exactly the needed distance from the previous toehold. It behooved us to follow closely in their footsteps if we were to make it to the top. Traveling straight up seldom slowed their conversation as they related stories of their illustrious past, customs, and folklore. At the same time their ears and eyes were open to nature around them. Because of the link with their animistic past, when their beliefs centered around nature, they still recalled and listened for the sounds along the trail. Often our pastor would dart off with lightning speed through the brush or up a cliff when he spotted movement. He might come back with a snake of high monetary value to be sold for Chinese medicine on the plains.

On the upper trail to Haucha, Pastor Peng told us of the lower trail we would experience in the dry season. It would cut the walking time in half by fording the river five times. When we experienced it, we found it to be a challenge every time. When the water was to our knees, which was seldom, we had little trouble. More often it reached our thighs and waists. At first we removed our shoes, but multiplying this by five was too time-consuming, so we learned to keep them on. Besides, they provided a better grip.

Once, one of the Chinese doctors with us was crossing, holding his shoes high in his hands out of the water. Suddenly he slipped and his shoes were lost in the current. Unfortunately, it was just about dark and we were unable to find them. Dr. Huang had to walk the remaining hours out of the mountains in only his socks.

In a letter to my parents, I described this river crossing. We had visited in eighty homes and seen more than two hundred patients. Although we had had deluges of rain before and during the clinics and experienced many landslides on our trek in, we had decided to risk the river road. I quote from the letter: "Going down the mountain was slick traveling. One slip and we'd have gone over the edge. God protected, though, and we arrived at the river to find it above our waists. Each time we crossed we formed a human chain. If one of us went down, we all had to pull for dear life to get that one up. The river floor was rocky and slippery. At one point my legs were separated by a boulder, and with the force of the water I couldn't get them together again. So I just kept doing the splits. The more I tried to bring my legs together, the wider they split. . . . It was a frightening experience to fight tons of water, but I released my tensions by laughing. After our last crossing, were we ever glad to hear the sound of the

121

Toyota in the distance. We knew Harry had made it through to pick us up."

Often Pastor Peng and others spoke to us of the need for a bridge across that river. Many had drowned trying to cross it during high water. The upper trail was long and tedious; and since Maer village was moving to another place, the upper trail meant many extra miles of trail for the Haucha people to maintain. Besides, getting the sick and produce out by the upper trail was so much more difficult. The need was often spoken as a sigh, or perhaps a prayer. We ourselves had experienced the treachery of the river at all seasons, and had seen the poverty of the village, but could offer the mountaineers little in terms of hope for a bridge.

Missionaries help heal hurts, give spiritual advice, and help build churches, but hope for a bridge? Each time we crossed, we also sighed for a bridge and prayed for God's infinite timing to make it possible.

Ruth Winslow gives health care instructions.

Missionary Harry Winslow baptizes a tribal Christian.

Crossing the gorge — every step must be sure!

123

Exhausted hikers pause briefly. Note missionaries Dave Williams, Ruth and Harry Winslow.

Chapter 16

To Meet the Need

Haucha had three major areas of need: The health needs of the people, the economic situation, and the problem of communication. The children, especially, had a high mortality rate from diseases related to malnutrition and the absence of family planning. Children and adults suffered from a high incidence of tuberculosis and other chronic related lung diseases. Almost all of the children had ear infections, gum diseases, and parasites. In most cases, all had learned to live with their pain as part of life.

Economically, there were few cash crops, other than the picking of a special pod from a tree in the interior mountains which could be used by the plastics industry. Most of what the people produced on their narrow, rocky, terraced fields was for self-consumption. Their land was tax free, but would not continue to be so indefinitely. It was imperative to get some cash crops so that the people would be able to pay land taxes, instead of forfeiting their land. Many of the young people were disillusioned with the remoteness of the village and wanted to move to urban areas.

The major problem for Haucha was communication. Because of the difficult steep trails and remoteness, the only solution to the problem was to move the village out to an area that could be better developed. The government had done this successfully for several other villages, and had a site about twenty miles north picked out for Haucha. Other villages in Wutai were not only getting roads, but electricity, telephones, and new schools. Each family had been urged by the government to pay $20 (U.S.), and to provide a certain number of days of labor for carrying in the power poles and lines. But there was no way the poles could be carried to Haucha, nor a road built to that remote spot.

Haucha's school was the poorest in the district. Teachers hated the hiking distance, so often the poorest or those needing disciplinary action were sent to Haucha. Later, however, a wonderful group of mountain young people were trained to teach in these schools. And the people of Haucha became even more resistant to moving from their beloved village of hundreds of years.

When I began to work in the Wutai District, there was little available health service. One government-trained doctor, Dr. Du, for an area of thirty-five hundred people lived in the central capital village of Wutai. He was busy with the families in that village, and also involved in politics. Often patients from other villages would walk a long distance to see him, only to find that he was out of medicine or not there. Working with him were several public health nurses who seldom left Wutai. While each village did have a trained midwife, with a sixth grade level of education, most had been trained during the time of the Japanese occupation, and few had had refresher courses. At Dr. Du's invitation and with his help, I was able to obtain a local public health nursing license. He was most supportive and grateful for what I could do for his people.

Well-baby clinics were the first step to health care. To put stress on prevention rather than cure was a challenge. We introduced soap in order to help prevent skin diseases such as impetigo. We taught the mothers to weigh their babies regularly and thus be able to gauge their own children's health. Incentive gifts, such as a bar of soap or a hygiene kit, were given when the weight gain was consistent and the baby disease-free. The gifts helped them make the change from the old ways to new childcare methods. Mothers' classes which demonstrated hygiene, preparation of baby food, and family planning were held in each village. When there were enough women to accept family planning, I would bring a doctor from the plains. Because I, their Teacher-Mother, had three children, this became the ideal number to have. But always there was that fear that because many might die, especially the boys, there should be lots of babies.

One day Teacher-Mother Winslow came with a "da dudz" (the literal meaning of this word is big stomach or pregnant). I had a red face and a lot of explaining to do. The next year many of the women had a fourth child also. For the most part, family planning was so successful that the elders of the village became alarmed, fearing for the propagation of the tribe.

A year and a half of monthly mountain clinics brought us to our first furlough in 1969. On our arrival in Seattle, I shared with Dr. David Williams my dream for regular mobile clinics to the villages in the Wutai District. He and his wife had been in Taiwan for two years, when he was serving the United States Air Force. They had visited the tribal churches and held a clinic. In 1970, he and his wife, Diana, felt led of the Lord to return for two years under Volunteers in Service Abroad (VISA). They lived in Pingtung and worked in the Pingtung Christian Hospital.

On his free weekends, we formed a team and ministered to the villages on a regular basis, making Pingtung Christian Hospital our base of operations. Dr. Du, the government doctor, participated in as many clinics as possible.

At first we tried to have a central clinic, but later

decided much more could be accomplished in terms of holistic care by visiting the people in their homes. Word would go around that the team was coming. The days we were in the village, the people would not go to their fields, but rather would wait for the team's visit. Often Harry or some seminary students were with us to counsel and pray if there were spiritual problems. In their homes we could visit the old grandmother sitting by the fire, coughing and spitting (likely tubercle bacilli); the next generation, perhaps a father with a peptic ulcer; and then the tiny baby with diarrhea swinging in a basket from the rafters. If the day was bright with sunshine, we could examine them best in the courtyard outside the home. From early morning to late at night, from the top of the village to the bottom, we would wend our way along those cliff dwellings, examining, smiling, touching, comforting, and sharing God's love.

Sometimes a group of Christian fourth- and fifth-year medical students would take their holiday weekend to join us, getting away for a time of combined practical experience and Christian ministry. They were always enthusiastic and helpful.

After two years Dr. Williams left to take an assignment in India. I was without a doctor. But the Vietnam War was in progress, and Kaohsiung was a port city for rest and recreation of United States Navy and troops. A Free Methodist chaplain was interested in exposing his doctors and dentists to some other diseases than what they saw on a navy ship. His contacting me for ideas about how I could involve them was an answer to my prayers. After Dr. Williams left, I had felt my limitations as a nurse. A public health nurse can do much in follow-up, but the time comes when she must have medical advice for her patients. The Lord always provided a navy ship just when I needed help, and my drug supply replenished.

On one trip to Haucha, the navy dentists saw 180

patients and extracted 160 teeth from sixty people. They gave lectures to the schoolchildren, and distributed two hundred toothbrushes. Because Haucha didn't have electricity, the clinic was held out in the school yard during sunlight. In one day the location of the dental clinic moved four times to keep up with the sun. A Navy reporter said:

> The Americans were surprised by the ability of the children as well as the adults to show no evidence of discomfort. In one case Dr. Post administered anesthesia to a third grader, and removed ten abscessed teeth in fifteen minutes with absolutely no hint that the child felt pain. They're made of something stronger than we are.[7]

Another comment I often heard from the American men was:

> Here we are with all our little problems, and they are up there hurting . . . they must be living in tremendous pain and they're happier than most of us. . . . I had the feeling that maybe what we were doing was like feeding the birds, and then going off and leaving them.[8]

We, in God's work, never felt like we were feeding and leaving them. We always felt that something valuable had been left in their hands. We prayed that with each pill and drop of cough syrup, a channel of God's love would flow. We also felt blessed by their grateful response.

In facing the economic needs of the villages, we looked to the government for help. The village had not reached a decision to move. The younger generation saw no alternative, and the older generation could not understand the dissatisfaction of the younger.

129

In the meantime, we asked an agricultural adviser, working with the Asia Vegetable and Research Center in Tainan, to come to Haucha and give advice to the farmers. He took soil samples and came back with the report of which crops would grow best and be cash crops. He gave workshops on rotation, compost piles, and other problems they might face. Best of all was his advice to plant pear trees and macadamia nut seedlings. The village as a community was able to gather enough cash to plant several thousand trees, and the church matched this amount. The Asia Vegetable and Research Center was so impressed with Pastor Peng and his desire to help his people that, after he spent several weeks at the institution learning farming principles, the center gave him several hundred macadamia nut seedlings.

The project had an excellent beginning, but a year or two later a devastating typhoon ripped through the valley, uprooting 50 percent of the macadamia nut seedlings. Afterward, Pastor Peng planted large quantities of coffee seedlings.

Marketing beautiful beadwork, a dying art, also helped to bring added cash to the families. The cash provided incentive to the older women to instruct the younger ones in the age-old art of needlecraft beading and cross-stitchery.

The problem of communication will be discussed in the next chapter. How beautiful God's plan is for His people, and how wonderful to see Him use people who are open and sensitive to Him.

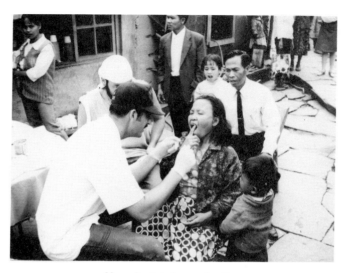

Navy dentist plans extraction.

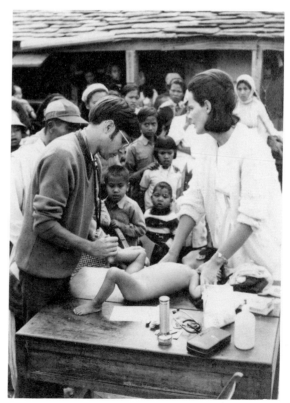

Navy doctor
examines baby,
assisted by
Ruth Winslow.

Chapter 17

Snakes, Green Berets, and Bridges

The snake lay coiled in the darkness waiting for its victim. The ledge, a few feet above the trail, provided perfect cover. The night sounds were cicada, mingled with the muffled voices of the villagers preparing for sleep. Jyamu village, perched high on the side of the mountain, is surrounded by eucalyptus trees, whose leaves rustle as the wind funnels up from the valley below.

Sensing no danger as we walked single file down the path, we were discussing the meeting just held. We were looking forward to a night's rest after a long day of clinic work.

Suddenly, the waiting snake lunged off the ledge and fastened its fangs into the heel of Miss Ba. His load of venom released, he slithered off into the shadows of the trees and bushes to safety. Miss Ba's cry, in her own tribal language, pierced the quiet of the night and caused us all to stop dead still. We were mesmerized by fear, knowing danger lurked in the darkness.

The first person to move was Dr. Du. Like a wound-up spring, he darted into the darkness after the snake with a stick and a piece of slate. Catching it was imperative. The mountains of southern Taiwan have many species of poisonous and nonpoisonous snakes.

Dr. Dave Williams, who was with us at the time, began to administer first aid. His problem was that he had a minimum supply of emergency drugs in his bag.

Early that same morning in February, our medical team comprised of three doctors, two nurses, several Christian medical students, and a United States Army Colonel, had set out early for several of the villages for a week of clinics. Colonel Shepherd was a personal friend of Dr. Williams, and had come along to observe and be with his friend.

By now we had the Toyota Landcruiser and could drive partway on the newly constructed road. We had been met by guides and porters and had begun the first clinic in Jyamu. Part of the team had left to go to another village, and we were planning to rendezvous together a few days later for a combined clinic. Our clinic was the only medical help these people would receive for awhile, and our spirits were high with anticipation of what God would do through us.

Miss Ba, the mountain nurse, had agreed to go along to help interpret; and I was the other nurse, going to hold classes in childcare for the mothers.

In the first village of Jyamu there had been an unusual lack of response to the gospel. Even though the stream of patients had been steady all day and into the evening, we had sensed a spiritual coldness. After a quick meal, the student pastor, attempting to work with the Christians, had called a home meeting. Slides on the life of Christ were shown by the students and they had given personal testimony to what Christ meant to them. There was little response. Could it be they had lost their once fervent love for Christ?

A year before, the old Presbyterian church had been torn down and never rebuilt. Meeting in homes, the Christians had gradually decreased in numbers, until only a few remained to make up the Jyamu Presbyterian Church. We had been pondering this as we walked down the trail when the snake had struck.

Miss Ba's cry carried far into the village. First to arrive was the village policeman. Without hesitation, he knelt with Dr. Dave to take his turn sucking the heel, where the incision had been made to try to remove the venom. Colonel Shepherd whipped off his belt to provide a tourniquet for her leg. Out of the darkness the people came running as the word spread. Women and children, young and old, were concerned for their own mountain nurse who had come to help them, who now had been struck down by the deadliest danger of all, a poisonous snake. With neither electricity nor refrigeration, antivenin was not available. Soon Dr. Du returned with the snake dangling, the head crushed.

"It is a hundred pacer," he quickly said. Murmurs of consternation were followed by the low wail, which always accompanies death. Miss Ba, having grown up in these mountains, knew that she had only moments to live. Her voice mingled with the villagers in the wail of death, but on her lips were the words, "Jesus, save me."

This much-feared snake is aptly named, because its neurotoxic bite allows the bitten victim to walk one hundred steps; and then with the vital nerves paralyzed, he dies.

Our reaction was not only one of furious activity, but wonder that such a thing could happen. Were we not special servants of God, protected from dangers, seen and unseen? We had prayed for protection that day as we started out. We had seen many snakes along our pathways and heard plenty of rustlings. Now, our thoughts were that God had permitted the accident for a reason as yet unknown to us.

By this time almost everyone from the village was there, surrounding the nurse's litter. We watched a miracle begin to take place. Gradually, replacing the death wails were pleas for God's mercy.

Would He please forgive them — forgive the coldness that had come over them and relight the fires of love they once had had for Jesus Christ?

"And please, God, save the life of our own dear mountain nurse, who came to help us." Over and over they pled for God's mercy. The prayers subsided. In that moment we knew that God's hand was in the apparent tragedy. We knew that He, not the snake, would triumph.

Quickly her litter was prepared. Two medical students were chosen to accompany her, Dr. Dave, and the four litter bearers down to the plains and the hospital. They moved quickly over the mountain trails, holding reed torches in their hands to light the way. The trail is bad by day, but by night it is treacherous. The drops into the valley are hidden and steep. To cross the rotten swinging bridges in daylight is unsafe enough, but by night each step is one of faith. The trip earlier had taken four hours in daylight, now by night it took three. Such was the speed of the litter bearers. Each minute was vital, and stops were made only to loosen the tourniquet and administer more sedative to the patient.

When they reached the car, it was Dr. Dave's turn to take the mountain road by faith, as he rushed around corners on two wheels and over bumps as though with no wheels. If he had been afraid of the dark trail and the speed at which the mountain men ran over it, now it was their turn to feel fear as the missionary doctor accelerated, causing them to hit the roof of the car on each bump.

At last they arrived at the Pingtung Christian Hospital and the Provincial Hospital where the antivenin was stored. The snake was analyzed and found not to be the hundred pacer, but one a little less deadly, the Taiwan habu. This one is hemotoxic, and allows the victim a longer time before the venom begins its deadly work.

A few hours later Miss Ba passed the crisis. Dr. Dave slept for a few hours, and before dawn left home again to rejoin the team, reporting the miracle that she would recover. Our clinic continued throughout that day and on into the week. In time, because of the spiritual awakening of the Jyamu Christians that night, they rebuilt their church and today have a strong Presbyterian church in that village. But the high drama from that night resulted in another miracle, which would take place within the year.

The remainder of the trip was comparatively uneventful. We treated a few hundred patients and everyone worked hard. Colonel Shepherd was an active member of our team. Driving out of the mountains, he sat between Dr. Dave and me on the front seat of the Toyota.

"Is there anything that our group of Army men could do to help in your work?" he asked. He had been impressed, not only with the way God had worked in saving the life of Miss Ba, but he had also seen the tireless work of Dr. Dave and the others, combined with a real love for God in ministry to the whole man.

The thought of a bridge came into our minds, but dare we ask for a bridge? This was the unspoken message passing between Dr. Dave and me. A bridge, a bridge, a bridge? Dare we, dare we, dare we? Could such a thing ever be? Then the question was out. We didn't know how or when but this was the one big need which might conceivably be accomplished by a group of Army men.

Without hesitation, Colonel Shepherd answered and said that he thought it could at least be looked into as a feasible project for his Green Berets. He was certainly high enough in the chain of command to bring such a project into being. The Green Berets had been the elite fighting men in Vietnam. Later they were removed as fighters and returned as training men to help rebuild their image. Instead of fighting, they were involved in building projects helpful to the Vietnamese people. It was a group of engineers stationed in Okinawa he had in mind when he committed men from the United States Army to building a bridge for Haucha village. A few weeks later, a team of men flew down from Taipei by helicopter to see the need and review it as a possible project.

During World War II the first phase of the road across Taiwan had been begun at Shweimen, and following the river the road had pushed several miles into the mountains. A cement bridge had been built, but both road and bridge had been bombed by the Allied forces. Besides mountain people, United States prisoners of war had worked on that project. Now twenty-seven years later, an American group was coming back to rebuild the bridge the Allies had bombed.

In many places the road was little more than a trail. The Taiwan government was just not interested in rebuilding the bridge and road to Haucha. They wanted instead to relocate the entire village far away. That was the plan, but no one in Haucha had agreed. An alternative was needed.

A few miles beyond the site of the proposed bridge was a large level plateau, thirty feet above the river. Here, a hundred years before, battles between the Paiwan and Rukai tribes had taken place. After fording the river five times and just before the steep four-hour climb to Haucha village, we would often rest by the last river crossing, and Pastor Peng would sigh. "This is where the village should be." It seemed like a possibility now. If a bridge were constructed across the river, the government would be much more in favor of moving Haucha to a closer site, still within reach of the farmers' fields.

A few months later the project had the approval of the United States Armed Forces in Taiwan, to be carried out as a Civil Affairs Activity Program project

(CAAP). Taiwan's Ministry of National Defense also gave its approval, and would provide a liaison officer from the Chinese Army to coordinate and assist in solving problems at the site. It also made available trucks and drivers for transportation of materials to the bridge site.

Funding for the project would be provided by the USARPAC/CAAP, and the Provincial Government would allocate a sum to match the CAAP amount. All labor would be provided free by the mountain people of Haucha. Taiwan Christian Service would help provide food for the workers at the site. I would coordinate the workers from Haucha to the needs of the Green Berets. Work would begin during the dry season, and would be completed before the rains began in April.

Excitement was in the air as the entire village of Haucha came down to the river for the official opening ceremony. One hundred women were dressed in full beaded costume. The Provincial Government headman from the Wutai District and Pingtung was there. Four United States Army Green Berets from Okinawa, Mr. Paseman, their representative, and I stood along the rocky shore of the river. Several beautiful mountain girls in full tribal regalia sang. Speeches were given, and the plan of work explained to the workers.

I remember standing there in the hot December sun with tears stinging my eyelids. What a direction my part-time missionary career had taken! I knew that for the next several months it would be a full-time job coordinating the labor force to get that bridge built.

Right then I basked in the goodness of God. He had allowed the apparent tragedy of a snake bite to move the heart of an army colonel, to bring to reality a bridge.

In the coming months, I had little time for writing. I did, however, keep the weekly letters going across the sea to my parents. In those letters I shared my tears, my problems, and my joys as I worked with our mountain people and the Green Berets, to see the bridge built to the glory of God.

Miss Ba, with Ruth Winslow close behind, hikes up a difficult trail.

Women in full tribal dress prepare to celebrate.

Green Berets camp at the bridge site.

141

Chapter 18

"Love and Courage, Your Daughter"

September 3, 1972

Dearest Mother and Daddy,

We hope to begin construction September 25. There is much yet to do before it actually begins. The road is still impassable for the military trucks. Jeeps and our Toyota have no trouble, but trucks loaded with sand could spell disaster. The villagers are working hard to widen the road. Dynamite has been brought in from Vietnam, and a guard of Chinese soldiers is watching it around the clock.

Yesterday Mr. Paseman and I hiked up to Wutai to make some arrangements. By the time we got there the man we went to see had already left the village. We must have passed him on the road. We felt low, because it had taken us hours to get there, and hiking in the heat of the day had made us tired and hungry. We accidentally bumped into the Peng brothers who cheered us up, and offered to help us find the man in Pingtung. So we had nothing to do but set off down the mountain again. Just before the offices closed we found our man. All the way to Wutai and back in a day. This was unheard of a few years back.

All I can think of is the prayer of Hannah: "For this child I have prayed." Dare I say bridge? So many have prayed.

November 28, 1972

The bridge was to have been started this Friday. All the workers are ready, tents are built, 250 bags of flour to make bread and 50 bags of rice are all under plastic. Now the chief engineer's father has died, so there will be another delay.

December 5, 1972

Another engineer has been sent from Okinawa, so with the opening ceremony on Monday, work will begin Tuesday. A helicopter of officials will fly in. The Toyota travels the river road very well now. I'll need to spend as much time at the river as I can, caring for any accidents and encouraging the project along. I'll bring the children as much as possible so they can get fresh air and sunshine. I expect this will be the highlight of my missionary career to date.

The bridge will be 240 feet long. The cable has been located in a San Francisco naval yard. Leave it to the Green Berets to scrounge around for what they need for building.

December 14

It is under way! A large retaining wall has been built. You should see the human chain, as rocks are passed from one to the other from the riverbed. Here the Army engineers are helpless. Only the mountain men, who have been building terraced fields for generations, are capable of fitting the rocks in place. The people are happy. Although their living conditions are not easy, they know it is temporary and for a good cause. Even children are taking their turn. Men and women lift equal loads, and put in equal hours from dawn to dark.

December 19

I'm at the river now. Sergeant Presler has been in-

144

specting the deep hole. I've learned this hole is the most important part of the whole bridge. In it will be poured cement which will hold the tons of cable. We need more dynamite. The chief engineer has just flown in by chopper to inspect the hole. There are four Army men here living on C rations and in tents. They seem to enjoy their work, and find the mountain people easy to work with and cooperative. They laugh and joke a lot. I spent several hours today with Peng helping him organize the village into work teams. Now that it is a reality, there must be people here all the time.

January 21, 1973

At the river. I got up at 4:30 this morning to come to the river and give the message that work would have to stop for the Chinese New Year's Celebration. Orders from the top, and just when the momentum is so good. There are fifty keeping busy now and another crew of fifty expected next week. What excitement for the mountain people.

The cement is to be flown in by Jolly Green Giant this week, and the cement mixer brought in on the road. Hope the road will take it. I think that a new master sergeant*, with a bit more experience, will be brought in after New Year's vacation.

It is raining now, and I'm sitting here under a cliff watching the river go by. Wish I had brought the children to play today. They would likely have fallen in the holes though. I am certainly learning a lot about bridges.

Now I'm sharing my shelter with several mountain people, who are joking and laughing, so I guess they aren't too low because of stopping work for ten days. I really feel one with these people and share their joy at the "golden" thing which is happening to them. Will close now . . . sorry for the smudges. I've moved to a drier spot now — hope you can read this letter.

*Sergeant Eugene Hall

February 27

The worst possible thing happened. No, I didn't go over the cliff, but the cement mixer did, killing one of the mountain workers. One of the holes had been filled with cement, so the contractor paid for it, and the cement mixer had just left the site. Because of that, we were not responsible for the accident. Five of the mountain people asked to ride the mixer out to Shweimen. About a mile from the river they started up a thirty degree grade. Halfway up the brakes failed. One side was the mountain and other the steep cliff. The driver yelled a warning and most of those riding jumped. But one old man, who was hard of hearing, didn't hear because of the roar of the motor.

The driver didn't have the presence of mind to run the mixer into the cliff side. He just let it go — and it went over the edge, taking the old man with it. It fell twenty-five feet and he was crushed. I helped to carry his body up.

The workers have asked for three days to mourn. They have all gone back to the village. I am absolutely numb that this has happened. We have prayed so hard for the safety of the people as they are around the heavy equipment. I will not question, though.

Later . . . I spent five days this week at the river. After the accident they all went up to mourn, but didn't return. The American Captain asked if I would go up there with him to recruit them back. He and I, and a little mountain boy left at noon. We went with wings on our feet, not stopping once. I think it was a record time of three hours. We met with the headman and Pastor Peng, and with their help were able to convince the people to come back. With one more hole to fill, we are at a vital place. It was too late to come back the same night, so we stayed with the pastor's family. It was a good experience for the American Captain.

On the trail, he entertained me with his Vietnam

146

War tales. I think that is what made me go so fast. With him on my heels, a real soldier, I had no choice. I did have some dizzy spells, but think it was because we traveled so fast.

On Friday, I carried twenty buckets of sand and helped with the digging, just to show them how much I care about the bridge getting built. This morning I can hardly move. My back hurts so. But I'll do it again next week for it's good exercise, and I feel more at one with the people when I can participate, rather than just supervise.

March 15, I think.

I have been interceding with the police, military liaison, mountain men, and the family about another death at the river. I feel as though I've lived a thousand years in the last two weeks. Yet I know, with the Lord giving me the strength, it has been a moment, an hour, a day at a time. When a project of this nature begins, we know we will have to pay the price. It will cost. At the time, we don't know just how much. That is where our faith and the reality of living with an unknown tomorrow comes into action. I was, and am willing to pay the price to see the project completed. More tears, as well as more blood, have now been shed.

The U.S. military men asked to borrow the Chinese Army dump trucks. These were World War II vintages, but still very suitable for the mountain road. Along with the trucks we had to take the Chinese military drivers, who were young and cocky. The rock and sand had to be carried down to the river where the bridge holes were already well reinforced with steel and ready for cement. Just before the holes is a sharp hairpin curve. The drivers had been told by their American counterparts, who had supervised the angle of this curve, that they would have to gear down to make it, and not under any circumstances try to make it in one turn.

About midafternoon one driver decided not to gear down. His truck was fully loaded and he didn't make the corner. There were workers all over. When the driver saw he couldn't make it, he shouted, jumped out and let the truck go over the mountainside. One dear old mountain man on the truck was crushed under the front as it landed upside down.

They drove him out in a jeep, called me at Shweimen, but I couldn't get to the hospital before he died. We had a quick meeting and decided to bury him there in Shweimen, rather than take him back through the bridge site to Haucha. The mountain people always bury their dead before sundown the day they die. Besides, we were worried that if we took him back through the bridge site, all the workers would want to accompany him back to the village; and then we'd have a hard time getting them all back to work.

The next day irate, distant relatives of the man, who lived in another far away village, came demanding a large sum of money for compensation. All workers had signed a release form that they wouldn't hold the Chinese government nor the United States military responsible for any accident. However, this man had come much later to work, and he had not signed.

We met in one of the work shacks for a grueling meeting with representatives of the Chinese Army, Mr. Paseman, village leaders, distant family members, and Pastor Peng. After four hours we were at an impasse. The pastor, and the village leaders were very embarrassed about the behavior of the family, and we felt their discomfort. We could pay a certain amount of insurance, but not the unrealistic sum they were demanding.

In the early afternoon Mr. Paseman stamped out. The Chinese Army representative, bored by it all, was reading his newspaper. The Chinese driver had already been sentenced to three years in military jail and no re-

148

tirement pay. It was hot and stifling, and I was very close to tears as Pastor Peng and I continued to remonstrate with the relatives.

Finally, I dramatically stood up and with Pastor Peng translating, and the tears flowing freely down my cheeks, announced that if they continued to press charges and write one thing against the United States and Chinese armies (which is what they had threatened to do by way of blackmail), the whole project would stop at once, even before the second tower was finished. Furthermore, I would not be able to continue to work among them, pay their hospital bills, take doctors to care for their sick, help them get electricity, or plant any more trees. I'm sure Pastor Peng added much to my words, for his translations went a lot longer than my short static sentences.

Then with one big sob, I, too, walked out of the meeting and joined Mr. Paseman on the other side of the river. He had a plane to catch for Taipei, and I was to take him to the airport. We sat in gloomy silence waiting for the rest of the group to come out.

Two hours later the family, who had tried to bolster their spirits with alcohol, staggered out. They asked us if we would take them to the village of Shweimen. But neither Mr. Paseman, nor I, felt like being alone with them in their inebriated states on the mountain roads. So we took off without them, leaving them in a cloud of dust, shouting "Syaujye, syaujye" (miss, miss).

Eventually, they dropped their charges. We gave more than the insurance plan, but wouldn't give it to the family. Settlement went through the pastor to the nearest relatives in Haucha.

Yesterday, I was at the river and watched fifty-eight people pour cement into the towers. I was so impressed. They didn't walk. They ran with their loads of sand and cement. As I watched and contemplated, it suddenly hit me what I had said and done to avert the lawsuit. My words may have averted the lawsuit, but they weren't spoken in the language of love. I would still have gone to them if they needed me. I would have continued to love and help them.

When the towers are poured, they will have to set for thirty days before the cables can be strung. We all need a break.

Love and courage

March 20

It is quiet at the river now. I've had numerous apologies from the people for the behavior of the distant relatives of the man who was killed. The towers stand tall and straight waiting for the cable.

April 15, 1975

In the meantime, I've discovered a lump in my breast and will be going to Taipei to have it removed. I may need radical surgery. You know all about that, Mother. Please don't worry. I haven't had it long. I have lost weight though. I am in the greatest Physician's hands. Yesterday, I bade farewell to the workers for awhile. I just had a feeling . . . .

More love and courage

April 27

You are anxious for news. So here it is. It was a nonmalignant lump. However, the other news is that there is new life within me. I'm pregnant again.

As you know, I was facing a very large mountain but now it seems like a molehill. During those waiting days, the agony was terrible, but yet I had peace. I determined to be a better mother and wife. Now the Lord has given me more time. I am praising Him. Never has the drive in on that mountain road seemed so lovely, or the river so aqua colored. Now I know why I was dizzy on the mountainside, and why my back ached so . . . no more buckets of sand. I am sure the people at the river will be delighted. However, it won't help my family planning clinics.

May 8

We had the ceremony for the opening of the bridge. It wasn't nearly as elaborate as the breaking ground ceremony. President Nixon is going to mainland China, so the government doesn't want any publicity on this project for the time being. There were no reporters. I wanted to have trumpets, brass plaques, and a great time of festivity. Instead, the whole village came, the Wutai officials, the dear army men and myself. The ceremony was low key.

Each army man was presented with a mountain knife in a hand carved wooden case. They were in full dress, as were the mountain men. I cut the ribbon.

After our last problem everything went smoothly. It was mostly the skilled American men out there on the cables, stringing the wires and laying the boards. It was dangerous work, though, and Sergeant Presler, my favorite, fell off the bridge and broke his ankle just before it was completed.

It is such a beautiful bridge. In spite of the times of discouragement and testing, I was able to cling to the promises of God. I'm a better and stronger person now for this experience. I've often sung the song, "Got any rivers you think are uncrossable? Got any mountains you can't tunnel through? God specializes in things thought impossible. . . ."

A bridge? Yes, it seemed impossible, yet God used people with faith to accomplish the impossible.

A chain of women carry gravel for the construction of the bridge.

Men pour concrete into the bridge tower mold.

A mountain youth helps happily with the new bridge.

One of the trucks missed the curve, but the Lord overcame the ensuing problems.

Chapter 19

New Haucha Village

The loads were always heavy! But going downhill with the goal of a new village and new homes, the loads became light. To build a new village and preserve the traditional decor was the project of the hour. So the houses were dismantled, with window frames, large slabs of slate for decorating, teak beams, and anything else that could be carried down the steep treacherous trail. Families worked together on the large cross beams. Going around the corners, and along the cliff edges required the skill and footing of a mountain goat. These capabilities, and the qualities of unity and togetherness, the people of Haucha possessed.

There was excitement in the air when I returned from our second furlough in 1978. The level plateau two miles beyond the swinging bridge had been bulldozed, and preparations for building the new homes had begun. Temporary shelters and tents were already occupied by the people.

The government had at last agreed to have the Haucha people move to the site of their choosing near the swinging bridge, but still within reach of their farmlands above. The government had been impressed with the community spirit by which the new bridge had been built, and had sent in surveyors to check the plateau for a possible new village site. In all respects the surveyors' report was affirmative. Furthermore, it was decided by the government to help the village become even more accessible; it would repair the road and build a cement bridge next to the swinging bridge. It had taken eight years of negotiations with the government — during which time the swinging bridge had been built — to bring it all to pass.

By now the disgruntled families of Haucha had already moved away, leaving eighty-seven families. The plateau was divided into eighty-seven lots, and these were drawn by the people. There was a large area reserved for the school and playground, meeting hall, police station, and public health station.

Each family would provide $800 (U.S.) for their new homes, while the government would give $500 to each. World Vision had also assessed the need and decided to match the government grants, provide basic furniture and cooking utensils, and supplying a food allowance while the people were building their homes and away from the fields. Cement and window frames would come from the government, and the people would collect their own rocks and sand. The latter was not a problem, as they had been building and terracing with stones for generations, and much of the slate from the old homes had been salvaged for the decorations on the outsides of the new homes. Each home would be traditionally tribal, and prizes would be given for the best decorated outside walls.

Strict sanitation rules were established from the beginning, with gutters and roads to be built even before the homes. The government also provided a contractor-adviser for every ten families, to ensure strong and safe homes. They had two years to complete the project. Then plans to help them agriculturally would begin.

One of the choicest sites was for the church, on the cliff overlooking the river and the mountainside. A temporary bamboo and straw structure was built even

154

before the homes, so that they would not be without a place to worship even for one Sunday. Pastor Ou was the appointed conference pastor at the time. He was a skilled mason and was able to help the people with their homes, as well as direct the construction of a beautiful church. The outside of this church was decorated with slate, cut into pieces and depicting the lost lamb. The shepherd was bending over a steep cliff to get the lamb on the ledge below. What a beautiful way to describe what Christ had done for these mountain people.

The Pingtung Christian Hospital was asked to provide health care for this new project. I was asked to join them, along with two Christian nurses, and Dr. Olaf Holen, a young Norwegian doctor. For me it was a continuation of my earlier work; but now, how much easier it was since we could go all the way by ambulance. Not quite! More often than not we had to stop and dig out the wheels. Here is a quote from my journal about one typical trip to Haucha:

"We had rain the day before yesterday, so the river isn't too full yet. However, the upper road beyond the swinging bridge is being worked on, so we had to take the river road. That meant fording the river twice. Dr. Olaf was fearful the brakes would get wet. They did, and at the second river crossing he asked us to get out to see if we could find a place to turn the ambulance around. Evidently he decided to take the risk and cross, but forgot his nurses were out looking for a good place to turn around. With a great splash he crossed, leaving us on the other side. There was nothing to do but start across. I thought I would be smart and jump the rocks. The others were smarter, and took off their shoes. You guessed it . . . I missed my footing and went down. The rest made it just fine. Dr. Olaf had a red face when we climbed back into the ambulance. The brakes were very wet. We made it up the steep grade and down into the village without brakes, but we kept the back doors of the ambulance open so we could jump out in case we didn't make it."

At first our clinic in the new village was held in a temporary tent, then in one of the homes, and finally in the new health station built by the government. There were three rooms, plus a bathroom, and a small place I could make into a darkroom for developing X rays. How different from our clinic days in the old Haucha village!

My journal records a typical clinic day in March, 1979. "I felt good and right about our clinic yesterday. Our main concern now is to get the thirty or more TB suspects X-rayed. We also need positive sputums in order for the government to pay for the expensive new drugs. Whether the government pays for the drugs or not, we will go ahead and give them at our expense. One lady with seven children, whom I have known for years in the old village, is a typical open case. We have put her on drugs and she has shown marked improvement. Now we are working on the children to get their X rays. They all have the same symptoms, but it is slow work.

"We had about twenty babies and children in the well-baby clinic for weighing. Each mother keeps her own Road to Health Chart, and is very happy when her baby follows the line upward in weight gain. This week we examined the fourth grade children and found many abscessed teeth.

"We had some excitement to spice up the clinic. We were called to the home of a patient to deliver her baby, and were preceded by a crowd of mothers who were in the baby clinic. When Miss He and I arrived at the hut, I was surprised at the number of shoes outside the door. (Mountain people always remove their shoes before entering homes.) We had to push our way to get to the patient's bed, on which there were three old crones sitting with their hands under the covers. Usurping their positions, we peeked underneath the covers to see a newborn baby on a dirty piece of plastic between her legs. There was still no afterbirth, but the baby was squalling. I shouted loudly for everyone to get out, which they did in a hurry. They were not used to seeing the usually placid Teacher-Mother Winslow angry. Then Miss He and I finished the job. Looking up a few minutes later, we noticed the room much darker. The crowd was peering in the window. I then realized that birthing, like dying, is a village affair in which they all have the right to participate. I brought the baby over to the window, and we admired it together.

"The new mothers are especially anxious for Dr. Holen's wife, who is also a doctor, to come up and take care of their family planning problems. We are using new techniques these days.

"Yes, I felt right about yesterday's clinic. Sometime I would like to measure our success. It isn't necessarily the numbers we have seen, it is touching lives. It is the quality of care we give. It is the way we feel as we give that care, which our dear people can feel through us. It is the love of Christ which makes us love them through medicine. That is our measure for success, the love given and received."

And so the story continues. On May 4, 1980, the new village of Haucha had its official opening and dedication. It was a moving experience for all who had worked so long and hard for Haucha village.

Present were the Magistrate of Pingtung County, many other important government officials, and those who had helped, including World Vision officials. The most important guest of honor was the Secretary of the Kuo Ming Tang party. This was the Year of Self-Reliance for Taiwan. The people of Haucha had again demonstrated their industrious natures, and their self-reliance.   157

That morning as the sun shone brightly dispelling the mountain mists, we who had worked for so many years to help Haucha village felt the dawning of a new day and a brighter tomorrow. There is still much to be done to help Haucha, as the villagers reclaim the surrounding mountainsides for fields, as well as work their old lands high in the mountains.

There is a challenge for the church as well, that it will keep its enthusiasm for Christianity, and the new ways that Christ has presented to the people. It is not enough to sit back and say that what we set out to accomplish has been accomplished, but we must continue to pray and support the people of Haucha with prayer and encouragement as they live and work in their new village.

Relocated village of Haucha of the Rukai tribe. The village was moved halfway down the mountains.

One of the many beautiful slate-decorated homes in new Haucha.

The trusty Toyota inches forward over a difficult stretch.

The new government-built bridge; to the left is the Beret-built bridge.

Epilogue

Following the spiritual vacuum that existed during the Japanese occupation, the mountain people were eager to accept the gospel in the early 1950s and 1960s. Thus resulted the exciting story of the early years of rapid Christian growth in two of Taiwan's tribes.

One of the main reasons for this success was the evangelization of the Rukai and Paiwan tribal villages, and the commitment to train early converts for full-time Christian service. Every one of the Free Methodist pastors written about in this book received a solid foundation in Bible-centered teaching and preaching at Holy Light Theological College. Besides these there are other Rukai and Paiwan pastors whose stories have not been told, but who are very much a part of the total picture of the mountain church. These pastors all witnessed the restlessness and demoralization of their people brought about during the Japanese era. They were ripe for receptivity of the gospel, and excitedly returned to their own villages to proclaim Christ. They have led the way for the development of a strong mountain church.

Unfortunately, there was a long period from the mid-sixties to the mid-seventies when few young people responded to the challenge of full-time Christian commitment. In the past few years, however, several

161

mountain young men and women have entered theological training. Among these is the daughter of Pastor Peng. She has now been graduated and is serving in the village of Wanshan. Her fiance will soon be graduated from Holy Light also. The nephew of Pastor Lo is another who has been graduated, and is pastoring with his young bride, a teacher, in Tawu.

The pull of materialism is strong among the mountain young people. Most have received at least nine years of Chinese education, plus three years of military training for the men. Television opened the window to materialism never before observed by their parents and grandparents. Industry sought their talents, providing the wages to make what they saw on television a reality. Thus, there is a whole generation of young people absent from the weekly church services in their home villages because they are working in factories on the plains. Furthermore, the young people have not experienced the many crises and conflicts their parents experienced under the Japanese; and they can only compare their present backward living conditions and culture to the materialistic, comfortable living in the cities. Our mountain conference realizes that this loss of potential leadership means loss to the church. The churches mourn the loss, along with the parents of the young people.

The more aggressive pastors, however, are meeting the need and going to the cities to hold weekly worship services for the mountain industrial workers. Pastor Lo keeps close touch with each young person from his church, and has made sure that if they don't get back home for worship, they at least send their tithes. Pastor Peng comes Sunday afternoons to Kaohsiung, where he has a service for Rukai factory workers. Urgent prayer is requested that these young people, who have migrated to the cities, will not lose their cultural identity and fall away from the faith. Pray that the pastors and laymen will see this as their mission field for expansion. There are approximately twenty-eight thousand tribal people now living in six major cities.

Before his conversion Pastor Ou was one of the early opponents of the gospel in Ali. After training, he ministered effectively for many years in the Wutai District. He went to be with the Lord in 1981. Peter and Esther Wu are now pastoring a church on the plains. God is using them. Most of the other Free Methodist pastors mentioned in this book are still working for the Lord in mountain villages.

In 1976 the Taiwan Annual Conference of the Free Methodist Church divided into three districts: the Rukai, Paiwan, and Plains, with each electing its own leadership. The pros and cons of this move are still being debated. Problems with leadership and unity are being prayerfully worked through for the best solutions.

Most of the mountain churches have been self-supporting within the districts for many years. However, the mountain pastors' salaries have not kept pace with the rapid increase in the cost of living. Some have combined secular work with their pastoral work to help meet family expenses. Pastors, wanting their children to have educational advantages, opt to send them to city schools. Mrs. Peng, for example, is presently working as a carpenter's assistant to pay the tuition fees of one daughter in nursing school and a son in industrial college. Even with her working, the Pengs have gone heavily in debt. Prayer is needed that the fires of evangelism will continue to burn in the hearts of our mountain pastors, who face spiritual apathy and growing materialism among their people.

Theological Education by Extension is one of the brightest spots today in our mountain story. Every Sunday dedicated Paiwan laymen and lay pastors gather in the Tsaopu church, more commonly known as the Miracle Church, for instruction in the Word.

Strong pastors, national professors at Holy Light, and most recently, missionary Wilma Kasten, teach courses in Christian education. Schoolteachers, farmers, men and women from different occupations, have been spending concentrated hours in study, which in turn is shared with their own village people. The new Tuban church is being pastored successfully by the vice principal of the Tsaopu Primary School. Pray that spiritual awakening and revival will take place, possibly led by laymen and women.

The story of the new Haucha village is still not finished. As the people have rebuilt their homes, built a new church, and begun to develop their land with the planting of custard apples, life has again become uncertain for them.

To supplement water needs for several million people in major cities on the plains, the government is planning, within the next several years, to construct a dam and water reservoir in the river valley above Haucha. If this plan develops, the new Haucha village will be submerged. The government has offered the villagers a site not far from the Three Harmony Village. This may mean another uprooting for Haucha.

Pastor Peng informed me in August, 1983, that he would spearhead the project. He was not at all dismayed. He was confident that God had allowed them the joy of building the bridge and then the subsequent move to the new site for many reasons which were good for his people. His optimistic spirit and loving concern for his people will be vital if the new project should become a reality.

The ministries of the tribal churches will continue, whether in the mountain villages or in the cities, where thousands of tribal youth are working. The tribal people are characterized by optimism and a great love for God. God, who has done a great work among these people, will complete it to His honor and glory.

Pastor Peng travels to Kaohsiung for Sunday afternoon services.

Ali church, nestled high in the mountains, often rings with singing.

Holy Light Theological College in Kaohsiung, Taiwan, is a source of training and inspiration.

166

Footnotes

[1] George Leslie MacKay, *From Far Formosa* (New York: Fleming H. Revell Co., 1895), pp. 13-14.

[2] Chen Chi-lu, *Material Culture of the Formosan Aborigines* (Republic of China: Taiwan Museum, 1968), p. 7.

[3] R. Ferrel, "The Formosa Tribes: A Preliminary Archaeological and Cultural Synthesis," Bulletin of the Institute of Ethnology, Academia Sinese, No. 21, 1966, p. 97.

[4] Alice Ballantine Kirjassoff, "Formosa the Beautiful," *National Geographic,* 37, No. 3 (1920), 273.

[5] Kirjassoff, p. 285.

[6] Kirjassoff, pp. 285-87.

[7] Paul Dewitt, "Navy Doctors' Medical Mission Is Labor of Love," *Navy Times,* June 21, 1976, p. 16.

[8] Betty Ann Smith, "Volunteers Hike to Hau Cha," *China Lantern,* March 19, 1976, pp. 4-5.

Bibliography

Books

Chen, Chi-lu. *Material Culture of the Formosan Aborigines.* Taipei: Taiwan Museum, 1968.

Copeland, Margaret. *Chi-oang, Mother of Taiwan Tribes.* Formosa: United Publishing Center, General Assembly of the Presbyterian Church, 1962.

Dickson, James. *Stranger Than Fiction.* Toronto: Evangelical Publishers, 1955.

Dickson, James. *He Brought Them Out.* London: Hazel, Watson, and Vincy, Ltd., 1956.

Dickson, Lillian. *These My People.* Grand Rapids: Zondervan Publishing House, 1959.

MacKay, George Leslie. *From Far Formosa.* New York: Fleming H. Revell Co., 1895.

Taylor, James H. II. *Entering the Open Door in Formosa.* Winona Lake, Ind.: Light and Life Press, 1956.

Whitehorn, John. *He Led Them On.* London: British and Foreign Bible Society, 1955.

Periodicals

Dewitt, Paul. "Navy Doctors' Medical Mission Is Labor of Love." *Navy Times,* June 21, 1976, p. 16.

Ferrel, R. "The Formosa Tribes: A Preliminary Archaeological and Cultural Synthesis." Bulletin of the Institute of Ethnology, Academia Sinese, No. 21, 1966, p. 97.

Kirjassoff, Alice Ballantine. "Formosa the Beautiful." *National Geographic,* March, 1920, p. 273.

Pierce, Bob. "Another Story I Shall Never Forget." *Missionary Tidings,* Sept., 1957, p. 245.

"Progress in Formosa." *Missionary Tidings, July-Aug., 1959, pp. 210-11.*

Smith, Betty Ann. "Volunteers Hike to Hau Cha." *China Lantern,* March 19, 1976, pp. 4-5.

Taylor, Alice H. "Tribal Evangelism." *Missionary Tidings,* Sept., 1955, pp. 262, 271, 279.

Taylor, James H., Jr. "On the Mountain Top." *Missionary Tidings,* Sept., 1956, pp. 265-66.

Williams, David. "The High Mountains." *Missionary Tidings,* Nov., 1968, pp. 3-7, 21.

Winslow, Ruth. "Born from a Bus Accident." *Missionary Tidings,* April, 1975, pp. 17-18.

Winslow, Ruth. "Snake in the Night." *Evangel,* Nov. 5, 1978, pp. 4-6.